Name ______________________ Class ______________ Date ______________

Skills Worksheet

Directed Reading A

AF249064

Section: Water in the Air

Write the letter of the correct answer in the space provided.

______ **1.** What is the condition of the atmosphere at a certain time and place called?
a. water cycle
b. humidity
c. weather
d. dew point

THE WATER CYCLE

______ **2.** What heats Earth's surface and causes water to change states?
a. moon
b. stars
c. equator
d. sun

______ **3.** What is the movement of water between the atmosphere, the land, and the oceans called?
a. condensation
b. weather
c. water cycle
d. evaporation

HUMIDITY

Use the terms from the following list to complete the sentences below.

humidity   vapor pressure   dew point

4. The temperature at which air is saturated is the ______________________.

5. The rate of condensation increases as ______________________ increases.

6. The amount of water vapor in the air is called ______________________.

Relative Humidity

Write the letter of the correct answer in the space provided.

______ **7.** What is a measure of how close the air is to the dew point called?
a. dew point
b. relative humidity
c. vapor pressure
d. weather

Measuring Relative Humidity

______ **8.** What does a psychrometer do?
a. It measures humidity.
b. It measures temperature.
c. It measures condensation.
d. It measures precipitation.

CONDENSATION

______ **9.** What is it called when a gas changes to a liquid?
a. evaporation
b. condensation
c. humidity
d. water vapor

______ **10.** When do liquid water droplets form?
a. when the air is saturated
b. when the relative humidity goes down
c. when the air is very warm
d. when the relative humidity is 50%

Dew Point and Condensation

______ **11.** What does NOT happen when ice cubes are added to a glass of water?
a. The temperature of the water drops.
b. The glass absorbs heat from the air.
c. The temperature of the water rises.
d. The cold water absorbs heat from the glass.

Reaching the Dew Point

______ **12.** What are water droplets that form on grass during the night called?
a. vapor
b. dew
c. hail
d. rain

CLOUDS AND PRECIPITATION

______ **13.** What is a cloud made of?
a. gases
b. warm air
c. water droplets
d. snow

______ **14.** What forms in a cloud when temperatures are below 0°C?
a. gases
b. water vapor
c. water droplets
d. ice crystals

Types of Clouds

______ **15.** How are clouds classified?
a. by their shape and altitude
b. by their altitude and temperature
c. by their shape and color
d. by their temperature and shape

______ **16.** Which of the following is NOT a cloud form?
a. stratus
b. air mass
c. cumulus
d. cirrus

Precipitation

______ **17.** Which best defines precipitation?
a. water changing into water vapor
b. water falling to Earth
c. water flowing across land
d. water going from Earth into the air

______ **18.** What is the most common form of precipitation?
a. rain
b. snow
c. sleet
d. hail

Name ______________________________ Class ______________ Date ____________

Skills Worksheet

Directed Reading A

Section: Fronts and Weather

Write the letter of the correct answer in the space provided.

______ **1.** What causes the weather to change?
- **a.** Earth warms up.
- **b.** Air masses interact.
- **c.** Clouds appear.
- **d.** The air vibrates.

______ **2.** What is a large body of air with the same temperature and moisture content throughout called?
- **a.** air mass
- **b.** front
- **c.** cyclone
- **d.** cloud

FRONTS

______ **3.** What happens when a warm air mass meets a cold air mass?
- **a.** They usually mix together.
- **b.** The warm air rises.
- **c.** The cold air rises.
- **d.** They always remain apart.

______ **4.** What is the area where different air masses meet called?
- **a.** front
- **b.** tornado
- **c.** severe weather
- **d.** condensation

Cold Fronts

Match the correct description with the correct term. Write the letter in the space provided.

______ **5.** Warm air moves over cold, denser air.

______ **6.** A cold air mass meets a warm air mass, but both air masses remain separated.

______ **7.** A warm air mass is caught between two colder air masses.

______ **8.** Cold air moves under warm air, pushing the warm air up.

- **a.** cold front
- **b.** warm front
- **c.** occluded front
- **d.** stationary front

Match the correct description with the correct term. Write the letter in the space provided.

_____ **9.** drizzly rain; then clear, warm weather

_____ **10.** many days of cloudy, wet weather

_____ **11.** heavy rain or snow

_____ **12.** cool temperatures; large amounts of rain and snow

a. cold front
b. warm front
c. occluded front
d. stationary front

AIR PRESSURE AND WEATHER

Write the letter of the correct answer in the space provided.

_____ **13.** What kind of air pressure does a cyclone have?
a. lower than surrounding areas
b. higher than surrounding areas
c. sinking air pressure
d. increasing air pressure

_____ **14.** What happens as the air in a cyclone's center rises?
a. The air loses energy.
b. The air cools.
c. The air sinks.
d. The air gets warmer.

_____ **15.** What are areas of high pressure called?
a. dew point
b. cyclones
c. lightning
d. anticyclones

_____ **16.** What kind of weather does an anticyclone bring?
a. humid
b. snowy
c. dry and clear
d. cloudy and wet

THUNDERSTORMS

_____ **17.** Which of the following best describes a thunderstorm?
a. heavy snow
b. cold and dry
c. strong winds, heavy rain, and lightning
d. decreasing humidity

______ **18.** Which of the following is a condition that produces a thunderstorm?
a. cold air near Earth and an unstable atmosphere
b. warm, moist air near Earth's surface and an unstable atmosphere
c. cold air high in the atmosphere
d. dry air and a stable atmosphere

______ **19.** Which kind of cloud makes a thunderstorm?
a. stratus
b. cirrus
c. cumulus
d. cumulonimbus

Lightning

Use the terms from the following list to complete the sentences below.

thunder lightning

20. The electric discharge between two clouds is called ______________.

21. The sound caused by air rapidly expanding along an electrical strike is called ______________.

TORNADOES

Write the letter of the correct answer in the space provided.

______ **22.** What is a tornado?
a. a rapidly, spinning column of air that touches the ground
b. a rapid expansion of air
c. a brief, light shower
d. a sudden, severe thunderstorm

______ **23.** How does a tornado begin?
a. The air is cool and dry.
b. A funnel cloud forms.
c. Winds make a layer of air spin.
d. Lightning releases energy.

HURRICANES

______ **24.** Which of the following best describes a hurricane?
a. a spinning column that touches the ground
b. a rotating tropical system with winds of 120 km/h
c. a funnel cloud
d. the boundary between air masses

Where Hurricanes Form

______ **25.** Where do hurricanes form?
- **a.** over land
- **b.** over the Great Lakes
- **c.** over the Arctic Ocean
- **d.** over warm, tropical oceans

How Hurricanes Form

______ **26.** What happens when a hurricane moves over cold waters?
- **a.** The storm gets larger.
- **b.** The storm's wind speed rises.
- **c.** The storm moves quickly.
- **d.** The storm loses energy.

EFFECTS OF SEVERE WEATHER

______ **27.** Which of the following is NOT part of severe weather?
- **a.** drizzly rain
- **b.** hail
- **c.** flash floods
- **d.** high winds

______ **28.** What is the leading cause of weather-related deaths?
- **a.** lightning
- **b.** thunder
- **c.** flash floods
- **d.** high winds

______ **29.** What is a storm surge?
- **a.** strong winds and hail
- **b.** a rise in sea level during a storm
- **c.** a low-pressure area
- **d.** heavy rain

SEVERE-WEATHER SAFETY

______ **30.** What should you do during a flood warning?
- **a.** Go to the basement.
- **b.** Move to higher ground.
- **c.** Enter the floodwaters.
- **d.** Do nothing.

Skills Worksheet

Directed Reading A

Section: What Is Climate?

CLIMATE VERSUS WEATHER

Write the letter of the correct answer in the space provided.

_____ **1.** What kind of conditions vary from day to day?
- **a.** climate
- **b.** weather
- **c.** latitude
- **d.** elevation

_____ **2.** What are the average weather conditions in an area over a long period of time called?
- **a.** latitude
- **b.** temperature
- **c.** climate
- **d.** wind

FACTORS THAT AFFECT CLIMATE

Solar Energy and Latitude

_____ **3.** What does latitude measure?
- **a.** tilt of Earth's axis
- **b.** heat from the sun
- **c.** distance from the equator
- **d.** air temperatures

_____ **4.** What affects the amount of direct solar energy at different latitudes?
- **a.** weather
- **b.** global circulation
- **c.** Earth's size
- **d.** the curve of Earth

_____ **5.** Why does the equator have high temperatures?
- **a.** The sun's rays hit it directly.
- **b.** It has more trees.
- **c.** It gets less solar heat.
- **d.** It has a higher latitude.

Latitude and Seasons

_____ **6.** What causes seasons to happen?
- **a.** the equator
- **b.** cold weather at the poles
- **c.** the tilt of Earth's axis
- **d.** shorter days

Global Circulation and Winds

_____ **7.** What does uneven heating on Earth's surface form?
- **a.** the four seasons
- **b.** streamlike movements of water
- **c.** lots of precipitation
- **d.** areas of different air pressure

_____ **8.** Which of the following statements is NOT true about winds?
- **a.** Winds affect the latitude.
- **b.** Winds affect the amount of precipitation.
- **c.** Winds carry evaporated water.
- **d.** Winds carry solar energy.

Topography

Use the terms from the following list to complete the sentence below.

rain-shadow effect   topography   elevation

9. The height of a landform above sea level is called ________________.

10. Air that passes over a mountain cools, and precipitation may fall. This is a process called ________________.

11. The sizes and shapes of the land-surface features of a region form ________________.

Proximity to Large Bodies of Water

Write the letter of the correct answer in the space provided.

_____ **12.** How does a large body of water affect nearby land?
- **a.** The temperatures have wide ranges.
- **b.** There is a rain-shadow effect.
- **c.** Temperature changes are sudden.
- **d.** Sudden temperature changes are rare.

______ **13.** What keeps California's temperatures moderate?
a. the Great Lakes
b. precipitation
c. the ocean
d. latitude

Ocean Currents

______ **14.** What are streamlike movements of water on top of the ocean called?
a. rain-shadow effect
b. surface currents
c. convection currents
d. dew point

______ **15.** What keeps the West Coast's temperatures cooler than inland temperatures?
a. air masses
b. Atlantic Ocean
c. California current
d. Great Lakes

CLIMATES OF THE WORLD

______ **16.** Why do different parts of the world have such different animals?
a. Animals adapt to only certain climates.
b. Animals cannot travel.
c. Climate does not affect animals.
d. Plants cannot live in arctic areas.

Climate Zones

______ **17.** Which of the following is NOT a major climate zone?
a. equatorial
b. temperate
c. polar
d. tropical

______ **18.** Which of the following is the coldest climate zone?
a. rain forest
b. tropical
c. polar
d. temperate

Name ______________________ Class ______________ Date ____________

Skills Worksheet

Directed Reading A

Section: Changes in Climate

Write the letter of the correct answer in the space provided.

______ **1.** Why do you not notice a change in climate?
- **a.** because people cause it
- **b.** because climate changes slowly
- **c.** because you cannot measure climate
- **d.** because climate never changes

ICE AGES

______ **2.** What happens during an ice age?
- **a.** Earth gets warmer.
- **b.** Ice moves toward lower latitudes.
- **c.** There is less ice on Earth.
- **d.** The sea level gets higher.

______ **3.** What happens during a glacial period?
- **a.** The sea level gets higher.
- **b.** There is less ice on Earth.
- **c.** Ice sheets get bigger.
- **d.** Ice sheets thaw.

CAUSES OF CLIMATE CHANGE

Changes in the Earth's Orbit and Tilt

______ **4.** What did Milankovitch say were the causes of an ice age?
- **a.** volcanoes
- **b.** changes in Earth's orbit
- **c.** the sun's cycle
- **d.** the sea level rising

______ **5.** What do the three factors of Milankovitch's theory change?
- **a.** the movement of the continents
- **b.** the amount of debris from asteroids
- **c.** the flow of air and moisture on Earth
- **d.** the amount of solar radiation received by Earth

Plate Tectonics

_____ **6.** What determines how much solar radiation a continent receives?
a. the continent's location
b. the continent's size
c. the continent's weather
d. the continent's humidity

The Sun's Cycle

_____ **7.** What powers most cycles on Earth?
a. volcanic eruptions
b. glacial periods
c. the sun's energy
d. asteroids

Asteroid Impacts

_____ **8.** What is an asteroid?
a. a mountain that may erupt
b. dust and debris
c. a small rocky object
d. part of the sun's cycle

_____ **9.** What is debris?
a. an ice age
b. high-energy radiation
c. a small rocky object
d. dust and smaller rocks

_____ **10.** How might an asteroid have caused the extinction of the dinosaurs?
a. It crashed into them.
b. Its dust blocked the sun.
c. Its orbit blocked the sun.
d. It made Earth hotter.

Volcanic Eruptions

_____ **11.** How do volcanoes change the climate?
a. Ash makes the land warmer.
b. Fire warms the air.
c. Dust blocks some of the sun's rays.
d. Ice forms at high latitudes.

Human Activity

______ **12.** What is a gradual increase in Earth's temperatures called?
- **a.** global warming
- **b.** ice age
- **c.** glacial period
- **d.** interglacial period

GLOBAL WARMING

______ **13.** What is Earth's natural heating process called?
- **a.** interglacial period
- **b.** glacial period
- **c.** ice age
- **d.** greenhouse effect

The Greenhouse Effect on Earth

______ **14.** Which of the following is a gas that causes global temperatures to rise?
- **a.** oxygen
- **b.** ice
- **c.** debris
- **d.** carbon dioxide

Consequences of Global Warming

______ **15.** What could happen because of global warming?
- **a.** Icecaps could form.
- **b.** Deserts could be drier.
- **c.** Sea levels could go down.
- **d.** Farming in Canada could fail.

What Humans Can Do

______ **16.** How can humans reduce pollution rates?
- **a.** by cutting down trees
- **b.** by turning up the heat
- **c.** by always driving automobiles
- **d.** by turning off the lights

Name ______________________ Class ______________ Date ____________

Skills Worksheet

Directed Reading B

Section: Water in the Air

1. The condition of the atmosphere at a certain time and place is called

______________________.

THE WATER CYCLE

2. What heats Earth's surface and causes water to change states?

____

3. What is the water cycle?

____

____

____

HUMIDITY

Match the correct definition with the correct term. Write the letter in the space provided.

______ 4. the temperature at which the rate of condensation equals the rate of evaporation

______ 5. the ratio of the amount of water vapor in the air to the amount of water vapor needed to reach saturation

______ 6. that part of total atmospheric pressure that is caused by water vapor

______ 7. the amount of water vapor in the air

a. humidity
b. relative humidity
c. vapor pressure
d. dew point

8. What does humidity depend on?

____

____

9. What happens when the rate of evaporation equals the rate of condensation?

____

____

10. When temperatures are below the dew point, what forms on a surface?

____

11. Explain how using a humidity sensor with a thin-film polymer measures humidity.

____

____

____

CONDENSATION

______ **12.** The process by which a gas becomes a liquid is called

a. humidity.
b. condensation.
c. water vapor.
d. saturation.

13. When is air saturated?

____

____

14. Why do water droplets form on the outside of a glass of ice water?

____

____

____

15. What is dew?

____

____

CLOUDS AND PRECIPITATION

16. What is a cloud made of?

____

____

17. What are two ways in which clouds are classified?

____

____

18. Name the three cloud forms.

____

____

____

19. Water, in any form, that falls to Earth's surface from the clouds is called

____________________.

20. Name the four major forms of precipitation.

____

____

____

____

Name ______________________ Class ______________ Date ____________

Skills Worksheet

Directed Reading B

Section: Fronts and Weather

1. What causes changes in the weather?

____

____

2. A large body of air that has the same temperature and moisture content throughout is called a(n) ______________________.

FRONTS

______ **3.** What usually happens when different air masses meet?
- **a.** Cold air rises.
- **b.** Warm air rises.
- **c.** The masses disappear.
- **d.** Air from the two masses mixes together.

______ **4.** The boundary between air masses of different densities is called a(n)
- **a.** surface current.
- **b.** cloud.
- **c.** front.
- **d.** anticyclone.

Match the correct description with the correct term. Write the letter in the space provided.

______ **5.** A warm air mass moves over a cold, denser air mass.

______ **6.** A warm air mass is caught between two colder air masses.

______ **7.** A cold air mass meets a warm air mass, but the two remain separated.

______ **8.** A cold air mass moves under a warm, less dense air mass.

a. cold front
b. warm front
c. occluded front
d. stationary front

9. Describe the typical weather brought by each front listed below.

Cold front: ____

____

Warm front: ____

____

Occluded front: ____

____

Stationary front: ____

____

AIR PRESSURE AND WEATHER

10. An area in the atmosphere that has lower air pressure than the surrounding areas and has winds that spiral toward the center is called

a(n) ______________________.

11. Areas of high air pressure are called ______________________.

12. How does a cyclone affect the weather?

____

____

13. How does an anticyclone affect the weather?

____

____

THUNDERSTORMS

______ **14.** What is an intense local storm that forms strong winds, heavy rain, lightning, and thunder called?

a. anticyclone
b. storm surge
c. tornado
d. thunderstorm

15. What two atmospheric conditions produce thunderstorms?

____

____

16. An electric discharge between two oppositely charged surfaces is

______________________.

17. The sound caused by air rapidly expanding along a lightning strike is

called ______________________.

TORNADOES

_____ **18.** What is a rapidly spinning air column with very high wind speeds that touches the ground?

a. thunderstorm

b. tornado

c. anticyclone

d. occluded front

19. When does a funnel cloud become a tornado?

____

____

HURRICANES

20. A large, rotating tropical weather system with wind speeds of at least

120 km/h is called a(n) ______________________.

21. Where do most hurricanes form?

____

____

____

22. Where does a hurricane get its energy?

____

____

23. Why doesn't California experience hurricanes?

____

____

____

____

EFFECTS OF SEVERE WEATHER

24. Name five things that are part of severe weather.

____

____

____

____

____

25. What is the leading cause of weather-related deaths?

____

26. A rise in sea level that forms in the ocean during a storm is called

a(n) ______________________.

SEVERE-WEATHER SAFETY

27. What is the most important safety measure during a flood warning?

____

____

Name ______________________ Class ______________ Date ____________

Skills Worksheet

Directed Reading B

Section: What Is Climate?

CLIMATE VERSUS WEATHER

_____ **1.** Weather conditions
- **a.** change from day to day.
- **b.** never change.
- **c.** change slowly over a long period of time.
- **d.** change every two weeks.

2. The average weather conditions in an area over a long period of time is

______________________.

3. What are the two main factors that determine climate?

____

____

FACTORS THAT AFFECT CLIMATE

4. Name the four factors that affect the temperature and precipitation rates of an area.

____

____

____

____

5. What does latitude measure?

____

____

6. Explain how latitude affects the temperatures at the poles.

____

____

7. What affects the amount of direct solar energy at different latitudes?

____

____

8. Explain why seasons happen.

____

____

____

9. What are the patterns of winds the result of?

____

____

10. How do winds affect climate and weather?

____

____

____

11. The sizes and shapes of the land-surface features of a region combine to form ______________________.

12. At high ______________________, the temperature of the air is lower.

13. Explain the process that causes a rain-shadow effect.

____

____

____

14. How does the ocean keep temperatures in California moderate?

____

____

____

15. Streamlike movements of water at or near the surface of the ocean are called ______________________.

16. What carries cold water from the northern Pacific Ocean south to Mexico?

____

CLIMATES OF THE WORLD

17. Why do polar bears live only in very cold arctic regions?

____

____

18. Name Earth's three major climate zones.

____

____

____

19. Why are there several kinds of climates within each of the three major climate zones?

____

____

____

Name ______________________ Class ______________ Date ____________

Skills Worksheet

Directed Reading B

Section: Changes in Climate

1. Why would you not notice a change in climate?

____

____

2. What two factors can make the climate change?

____

____

ICE AGES

3. What does the geologic record show about Earth's climate?

____

____

4. A long period when ice forms in high latitudes and moves toward lower latitudes is a(n) ______________________.

5. Periods of cold and periods of warmth during an ice age are called ______________________.

6. Why does the sea level drop during times when ice covers large areas of Earth?

____

____

CAUSES OF CLIMATE CHANGE

7. What does the Milankovitch theory explain?

____

____

____

8. What does a continent's location relative to the equator and poles determine?

____

____

9. What happens when continents move?

____

____

10. How does the sun's energy affect the amount of energy in Earth's system?

____

____

____

____

11. A small, rocky object that orbits the sun is called a(n)

______________________.

12. Dust and smaller rocks are called ______________________.

13. Explain how an asteroid could have caused the dinosaurs to become extinct 65 million years ago.

____

____

____

____

____

14. What happens during a volcanic eruption in which some of the sun's rays are blocked?

____

____

15. A gradual increase in average global temperatures is called

______________________.

GLOBAL WARMING

______ **16.** Earth's natural heating process, in which gases in the atmosphere absorb thermal energy, is called

a. global warming.
b. the greenhouse effect.
c. an ice age.
d. a glacial period.

17. What do many scientists think cause the rise in global temperatures?

____

____

18. List three possible consequences of global warming.

____

____

____

Name ______________________ Class ______________ Date ______________

Skills Worksheet

Vocabulary and Section Summary A

Water in the Air

VOCABULARY

In your own words, write a definition of the following terms in the space provided.

1. weather

____

____

____

2. humidity

____

____

____

3. dew point

____

____

____

4. relative humidity

____

____

____

5. condensation

____

____

____

6. precipitation

____

____

____

SECTION SUMMARY

Read the following section summary.

- The sun's energy causes water to change states and to move through the water cycle.
- The amount of water vapor in the air is called *humidity*.
- When the temperature of the air cools to the dew point, the air is saturated and liquid water droplets form.
- Clouds form as air rises and cools, which causes water droplets to form on small particles in the air.
- Precipitation is water, in any form, that falls to Earth's surface from the clouds.

Name ______________________ Class ______________ Date ____________

Skills Worksheet

Vocabulary and Section Summary A

Fronts and Weather

VOCABULARY

In your own words, write a definition of the following terms in the space provided.

1. air mass

____

____

____

2. front

____

____

____

3. cyclone

____

____

____

4. lightning

____

____

____

5. thunder

____

____

____

6. tornado

____

____

____

SECTION SUMMARY

Read the following section summary.

- Thunderstorms are weather systems that produce strong winds, heavy rain, lightning, and thunder.
- Lightning is a large electric discharge that occurs between two oppositely charged surfaces. Lightning releases a great deal of energy and can be very dangerous.
- Tornadoes are small, rapidly rotating columns of air that touch the ground and can cause severe damage.
- A hurricane is a large, rotating tropical weather system that has high wind speeds.
- In the event of severe weather, it is important to stay safe. Listen to your local TV or radio stations for updates, and remain indoors and away from windows.

Name ______________________ Class ______________ Date ____________

Skills Worksheet

Vocabulary and Section Summary A

What Is Climate?

VOCABULARY

In your own words, write a definition of the following terms in the space provided.

1. climate

____

____

2. latitude

____

____

3. elevation

____

____

4. surface current

____

____

SECTION SUMMARY

Read the following section summary.

- Climate is the average weather conditions in an area over a long period of time.
- The curve of Earth's surface affects the amount of direct solar energy that reaches the ground at different latitudes.
- The tilt of Earth on its axis causes the seasons.
- Winds affect the climate of an area by transferring solar energy and by carrying moisture.
- Topography influences an area's climate by affecting both the transfer of energy and the rate of precipitation.
- Large bodies of water and ocean currents influence the climate of an area by affecting the temperature of the air.
- The three main climate zones of the world are the tropical zone, the temperate zone, and the polar zone.

Name ________________ Class ________ Date ________

Skills Worksheet

Vocabulary and Section Summary A

Changes in Climate

VOCABULARY

In your own words, write a definition of the following terms in the space provided.

1. ice age

____

____

____

2. global warming

____

____

____

3. greenhouse effect

____

____

____

SECTION SUMMARY

Read the following section summary.

- Earth's climate has changed repeatedly throughout geologic time.
- The Milankovitch theory states that Earth's climate changes as Earth's orbit and the tilt of Earth's axis change.
- Climate changes may also be affected by continental drift, volcanic eruptions, asteroid impacts, solar activity, and human activity.
- Excess CO_2 is believed to contribute to global warming.

Name ______________________ Class ______________ Date ____________

Skills Worksheet

Vocabulary and Section Summary B

Water in the Air

VOCABULARY

After you finish reading the section, try this puzzle! In each of the following items, use the clue to unscramble the letters, and write the term in the space provided.

1. amount of moisture the air contains compared with the maximum it can hold at a given temperature: TIVEALER YTIDIMUH

____

2. water in solid or liquid form that falls from the air to Earth: CIPIPERATTOIN

____

3. amount of moisture in the air: DIMUHTIY

____

4. condition of the atmosphere at a certain time and place: EAWETHR

____

5. when water vapor becomes a liquid: OEAIOCNDNSTN

____

5. temperature at which the rate of condensation equals the rate of evaporation: EDW OIPTN

____

SECTION SUMMARY

Read the following section summary.

- The sun's energy causes water to change states and to move through the water cycle.
- The amount of water vapor in the air is called *humidity*.
- When the temperature of the air cools to the dew point, the air is saturated and liquid water droplets form.
- Clouds form as air rises and cools, which causes water droplets to form on small particles in the air.
- Precipitation is water, in any form, that falls to Earth's surface from the clouds.

Name ______________________________ Class ______________ Date ____________

Skills Worksheet

Vocabulary and Section Summary B

Fronts and Weather

VOCABULARY

After you finish reading the section, try this worksheet!

Donald Deluge is a storm chaser—a person who follows dangerous weather in order to observe and record its effects. He likes to report his observations over the radio from his storm-chaser van. Unfortunately, some of the words from his latest broadcast were hard to understand, and Don hasn't been seen since his last adventure, so he isn't around to clear things up. See if you can help by reading the transcript of Don's latest adventure and filling in the blank spaces with the vocabulary words listed below.

Vocabulary Words

- tornado
- front
- thunder
- cyclone
- air mass
- lightning

[begin transcript]
12:34 pm

It seems there is a large ______________________ to the north of our current position in which the warm temperature and high humidity of the air are

constant throughout. From the south, there is a cold ______________________

moving under this warmer area. Looking at the satellite images, there appears to be a low pressure zone in which air is spiraling in and forming a(n)

______________________. There's a lot of cloud cover forming there. Looks like we might get a nice-sized storm! I'll be in contact again once I get closer to the hot zone.

1:21 pm

I was right! We have a nice thunderstorm forming. Looks like a cold front has moved in over the mountains to the west, right on top of the warm mass. There's a lot of electrical energy in the air here. The cumulonimbus clouds must have an opposite charge than the ground surface because all kinds of

______________________ strikes are occurring around me. . . WOW! Did you

hear that ______________________? A tree right next to us just got hit! This storm is awesome! I'll be back in contact once we clear the tree from the road.

1:38 pm

A funnel cloud is forming above a field to the right of us. Looks like it is going

to touch down and we might have ourselves a(n) ______________________!

We're going to try to get a little closer. I'll be in contact again shortly.

[end transcript]

SECTION SUMMARY

Read the following section summary.

- Thunderstorms are weather systems that produce strong winds, heavy rain, lightning, and thunder.
- Lightning is a large electric discharge that occurs between two oppositely charged surfaces. Lightning releases a great deal of energy and can be very dangerous.
- Tornadoes are small, rapidly rotating columns of air that touch the ground and can cause severe damage.
- A hurricane is a large, rotating tropical weather system that has high wind speeds.
- In the event of severe weather, it is important to stay safe. Listen to your local TV or radio stations for updates, and remain indoors and away from windows.

Name ______________________ Class ______________ Date ____________

Skills Worksheet

Vocabulary and Section Summary B

What Is Climate?

VOCABULARY

After you finish reading the section, try this puzzle! In the space provided, write the term described. Use the clues below to fill in the correct term, then solve the word search puzzle below. Words in the puzzle are hidden vertically, horizontally, diagonally, and backward.

______________ **1.** the average weather condition in an area over a long period of time

______________ **2.** the condition of the atmosphere at a certain time

______________ **3.** the distance north or south from the equator

______________ **4.** the height of surface landforms above sea level

______________ **5.** a horizontal movement of ocean water that occurs at or near the ocean's surface

______________ **6.** the combination of the sizes and shapes of the land-surface features of a region

S	U	R	F	A	C	E	C	U	R	R	E	N	T
A	V	W	B	S	T	B	L	U	A	E	I	O	O
P	E	W	T	W	S	M	I	N	F	G	M	A	P
C	L	I	S	P	E	A	M	X	E	I	B	T	O
P	E	H	M	N	A	A	A	A	M	L	K	G	G
H	V	B	A	R	O	H	T	Y	E	B	B	L	R
S	A	C	B	I	O	N	E	H	E	A	C	M	A
F	T	T	C	A	H	D	I	D	E	I	O	G	P
H	I	S	L	E	G	L	M	O	S	R	E	R	H
P	O	N	B	A	F	E	S	M	B	R	A	S	Y
N	N	D	M	E	D	U	T	I	T	A	L	F	G

SECTION SUMMARY

Read the following section summary.

- Climate is the average weather conditions in an area over a long period of time.
- The curve of Earth's surface affects the amount of direct solar energy that reaches the ground at different latitudes.
- The tilt of Earth on its axis causes the seasons.
- Winds affect the climate of an area by transferring solar energy and by carrying moisture.
- Topography influences an area's climate by affecting both the transfer of energy and the rate of precipitation.
- Large bodies of water and ocean currents influence the climate of an area by affecting the temperature of the air.
- The three main climate zones of the world are the tropical zone, the temperate zone, and the polar zone.

Name ______________________ Class ______________ Date ____________

Skills Worksheet

Vocabulary and Section Summary B

Changes in Climate

VOCABULARY

After you finish reading the section, try this puzzle! The terms in parentheses have all lost their vowels and spaces. Use the clues to fill in the correct term in the space provided.

1. During ______________________, large sheets of ice advance, and the sea level drops. (GLCLPRDS)

2. Natural events and human activities can cause ______________________, which is a gradual increase in the average global temperature. (GLBLWRMNG)

3. When a large piece of rock hits Earth, ______________________ shoots into the atmosphere. (DBRS)

4. Earth's natural heating process is called the ______________________. (GRNHSFFCT)

5. Scientists have found evidence of many major ______________________ during Earth's geologic history. (CGS)

6. A small, rocky object that orbits the sun and sometimes crashes into Earth is called a(n) ______________________. (STRD)

SECTION SUMMARY

Read the following section summary.

- Earth's climate has changed repeatedly throughout geologic time.
- The Milankovitch theory states that Earth's climate changes as Earth's orbit and the tilt of Earth's axis change.
- Climate changes may also be affected by continental drift, volcanic eruptions, asteroid impacts, solar activity, and human activity.
- Excess CO_2 is believed to contribute to global warming.

Name ______________________________ Class ______________ Date ____________

Skills Worksheet

Reinforcement

Severe Weather

Complete this worksheet after you finish reading the section "Fronts and Weather." The table below will help you to compare and contrast the different kinds of severe weather. Fill in the table according to the directions.

1. Describe the conditions under which each storm is most likely to occur.

2. Describe how each storm forms.

	Conditions	Formation
Thunderstorm		
Tornado		
Hurricane		

Name ______________________________ Class ________________ Date ____________

Skills Worksheet

Critical Thinking

Cyberspace Heats Up

While surfing the Internet, you find a chat room about global warming. The participants are in the middle of the following heated debate:

ZED: I'm telling you people, global warming is a myth! I have exercised outside every day for the last 20 years and haven't noticed a change in temperature. The problem with people today is that they are too dependent on air-conditioning. They just think it's hotter outside because they're SPOILED!

Dr. Betty: Excuse me, your highness, but I work as an environmental researcher. I can tell you that global warming is a very real and serious threat. If you look at any almanac, you will find that the 1990s was the hottest decade on record and that average global temperatures continue to rise at a slow but constant rate.

Milhouse: But CO_2 is natural! We exhale it every time we breathe! Besides, extra CO_2 is just absorbed by trees around the world. This global warming stuff is a big conspiracy.

Lucy F: A conspiracy against hair spray! They want us to have limp, lifeless hair!

ZED: Dr. Betty, if global warming were exposed as a fraud, you'd lose your job.

USEFUL TERMS

almanac a book that contains facts about a given year
conspiracy a secret plan involving two or more people
fraud something said or done that is not truthful

EVALUATING SOURCES

1. Is the Internet always a reliable source of scientific fact? Explain your answer.

____

____

____

2. Which of the people chatting above has the most scientific point of view? Explain your answer.

____

____

____

____

ANALYZING A VIEWPOINT

3. Do any of these people show bias in their argument? Explain your answer.

____

____

____

____

APPLYING CONCEPTS

4. From what you know about global warming, what is wrong with Milhouse's argument?

____

____

____

____

EVALUATING SOURCES

5. What kinds of Web sites might offer more objective scientific information than chat rooms offer?

Helpful Hint

Internet chat rooms are typically open for the general public's use.

____

____

____

____

Name ______________________ Class ______________ Date ____________

Activity

SciLinks Activity

THE WATER CYCLE

Go to www.scilinks.org. To find links related to the water cycle, type in the keyword HY71626. Then, use the links to answer the following questions about the water cycle.

Internet Resources

For a variety of links related to this chapter, go to www.scilinks.org

Topic: Water Cycle

SciLinks code: HY71626

1. Where does water evaporate from?

____

____

____

2. What happens when water vapor in the sky cools and condenses?

____

____

3. Where does rainwater go?

____

____

4. What do rates of water evaporation depend on?

____

____

5. What is the greatest source of evaporated water in the atmosphere?

____

6. Describe the process of transpiration.

____

____

7. Explain what it means when water vapor in the air rises mostly by convection.

____

____

____

Name ______________________ Class ______________ Date ______________

Skills Worksheet

Section Review

Water in the Air

USING VOCABULARY

Use a term from the section to complete each sentence below.

1. ______________________ is the amount of water vapor in the air.

2. ______________________ is any form of water that falls to Earth's surface from the clouds.

UNDERSTANDING CONCEPTS

3. Summarizing Explain how relative humidity relates to the amount of water vapor in the air.

____

____

____

____

4. Describing Describe the four processes in the water cycle.

____

____

____

____

5. Summarizing What is the dew point?

____

____

____

6. Demonstrating What is the water cycle's energy source?

____

____

____

____

CRITICAL THINKING

7. Identifying Relationships What happens to the rates of condensation and evaporation as the air temperature drops below the dew point?

____

____

____

____

INTERPRETING GRAPHICS

Use the illustration below to answer the next two questions.

8. Making Inferences By its shape, name this type of cloud.

____

9. Evaluating Data Estimate the altitude of this cloud.

____

____

CHALLENGE

10. Identifying Relationships One body of air has a relative humidity of 97%. Another has a relative humidity of 44%. At the same temperature, which body of air is closer to its dew point? Explain your answer.

____

____

____

____

____

Name ______________________ Class ______________ Date ____________

Skills Worksheet

Section Review

Fronts and Weather

USING VOCABULARY

Use a term from the section to complete each sentence below.

1. A(n) ______________________ is a brief storm that consists of rain, strong winds, lightning, and thunder.

2. ______________________ is the sound caused by the rapid expansion of air along a lightning strike.

UNDERSTANDING CONCEPTS

3. Comparing Compare a cold front and a warm front.

____

____

____

4. Analyzing How does energy from the sun lead to the formation of hurricanes?

____

____

____

____

5. Evaluating What causes lightning?

____

____

____

6. Applying What type of weather would you expect a cold front to produce? a warm front?

____

____

____

____

7. **Applying** How do floods affect people?

8. **Applying** How do heat flow and air movement relate to the formation of thunderstorms?

CRITICAL THINKING

9. **Making Comparisons** Compare cyclones and anticyclones and the weather patterns that they cause.

10. **Identifying Relationships** Explain what happens to a hurricane as it moves over land.

11. **Identifying Relationships** How does severe weather cause floods?

12. **Identifying Relationships** Flooding can cause property damage and endanger human lives. Describe how flooding might affect wildlife habitats.

INTERPRETING GRAPHICS

Use the illustration below to answer the next two questions.

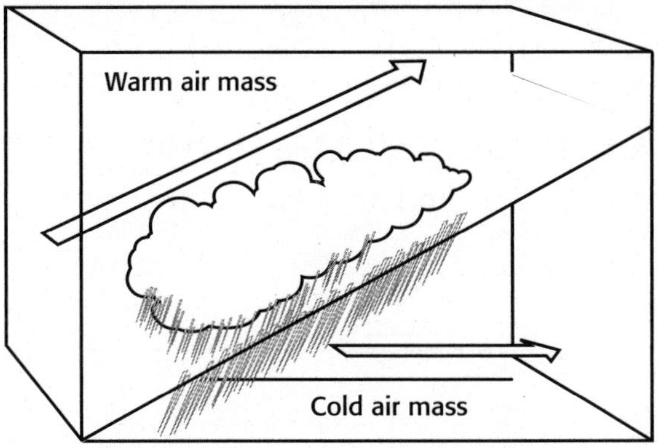

13. Analyzing Processes In which direction is the front moving? How can you tell?

______

______

______

14. Evaluating Data What type of front is represented in the illustration?

______

______

______

CHALLENGE

15. Applying Concepts Fronts form when two moving air masses meet. Explain what causes the air masses to move. What would weather be like if air masses did not move? Why don't fronts form between two air masses that have the same temperature?

______

______

______

______

______

______

______

______

Name ______________________ Class ______________ Date ____________

Skills Worksheet

Section Review

What Is Climate?

USING VOCABULARY

1. Write an original definition for *climate*, *latitude*, *elevation*, and *surface current.*

UNDERSTANDING CONCEPTS

2. Analyzing Explain how topography affects climate.

3. Comparing What is the difference between weather and climate?

4. Identifying Identify five factors that affect climate.

5. Evaluating Explain why there is a difference in climate between areas at 0° latitude and areas at 45° latitude.

6. Identifying What carries solar energy from one place to another in the atmosphere?

____

____

____

CRITICAL THINKING

7. Evaluating Data Describe what you think the climate might be like at the very southern tip of South America.

____

____

____

____

8. Applying Concepts During what months does Australia have summer? Explain your answer.

____

____

____

____

9. Predicting Consequences How would global climate be affected if Earth were not tilted on its axis? Explain your answer.

____

____

____

____

10. Analyzing Ideas Explain why climates cannot be classified only by latitude.

____

____

____

____

INTERPRETING GRAPHICS

Use the diagram below to answer the next three questions.

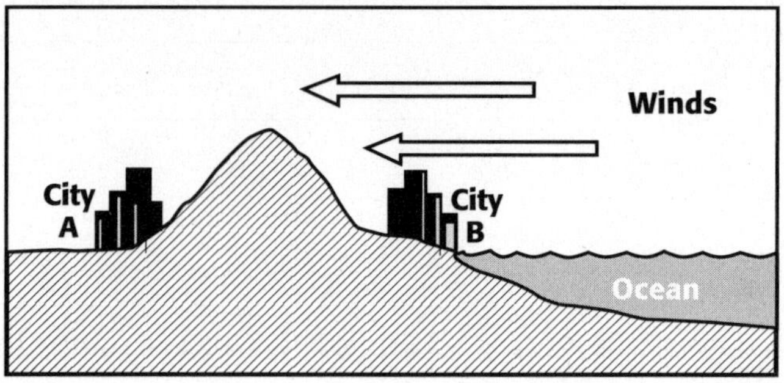

11. **Evaluating Data** Which city is more likely to have the largest yearly temperature range? Explain your answer.

____

____

____

12. **Applying Concepts** Which city is more likely to have a dry climate? Explain your answer.

____

____

____

13. **Making Comparisons** Describe the climates of each city.

____

____

____

CHALLENGE

14. **Applying Concepts** Describe how latitude, winds, topography, and ocean currents affect the climate of California.

____

____

____

____

____

Name ______________________ Class ______________ Date ____________

Skills Worksheet

Section Review

Changes in Climate

USING VOCABULARY

1. Write an original definition for *ice age*, *global warming*, and *greenhouse effect*.

UNDERSTANDING CONCEPTS

2. **Analyzing** How does the Milankovitch theory explain climate changes?

3. **Identifying** What factors affect the amount of solar energy that reaches Earth's surface?

4. **Concluding** Explain how global warming could cause flooding.

5. **Listing** List the factors that might cause changes in Earth's climates.

6. **Describing** Explain how the greenhouse effect warms Earth.

CRITICAL THINKING

7. **Analyzing Relationships** How would the warming of Earth affect agriculture in different parts of the world? Explain your answer.

8. **Applying Concepts** Describe how you could decrease the amount of CO_2 released in the atmosphere.

MATH SKILLS

9. Using Equations If burning 4 L of gasoline produces 9 kg of CO_2, and a car burns 160 L of gasoline in a month, how much CO_2 did the vehicle release during the month? Show your work below.

CHALLENGE

10. Predicting Consequences Can short-term climate changes over a 100-year period be explained by changes in the tilt of Earth's axis? Explain your answer.

Name ______________________________ Class ______________ Date ____________

Skills Worksheet

Chapter Review

USING VOCABULARY

______ **1. Academic Vocabulary** Which of the following words is closest in meaning to the word *affected*?

a. worsened
b. improved
c. influenced
d. moved

For each pair of terms, explain how the meanings of the terms differ.

2. *relative humidity* and *dew point*

____

____

3. *condensation* and *precipitation*

____

____

4. *air mass* and *front*

____

____

5. *weather* and *climate*

____

____

6. *thunder* and *lightning*

____

____

UNDERSTANDING CONCEPTS

Multiple Choice

______ **7.** Which of the following is a form of precipitation?

a. fog
b. cloud
c. snow
d. dew

______ **8.** Fronts that form when a warm air mass is trapped between cold air masses and is forced to rise are
a. snow fronts.
b. warm fronts.
c. occluded fronts.
d. cold fronts.

______ **9.** A severe storm that forms when a rapidly rotating funnel cloud touches the ground is a
a. hurricane.
b. tornado.
c. typhoon.
d. thunderstorm.

______ **10.** Which of the following would not be a threat to humans or their property?
a. hurricane
b. tornado
c. thunder
d. lightning

Short Answer

11. Comparing Explain the relationship between condensation and dew point.

____

____

12. Describing Describe the weather conditions along a stationary front.

____

____

13. Summarizing Explain how a hurricane develops.

____

____

14. Analyzing Describe the water cycle, and explain how it affects weather.

____

____

15. Evaluating Explain how wind patterns can influence climate.

____

____

16. Concluding How can severe weather affect humans and their property?

____

____

17. Identifying Name four factors that cause changes in weather.

____

____

____

____

INTERPRETING GRAPHICS

Use the graph below to answer the next two questions.

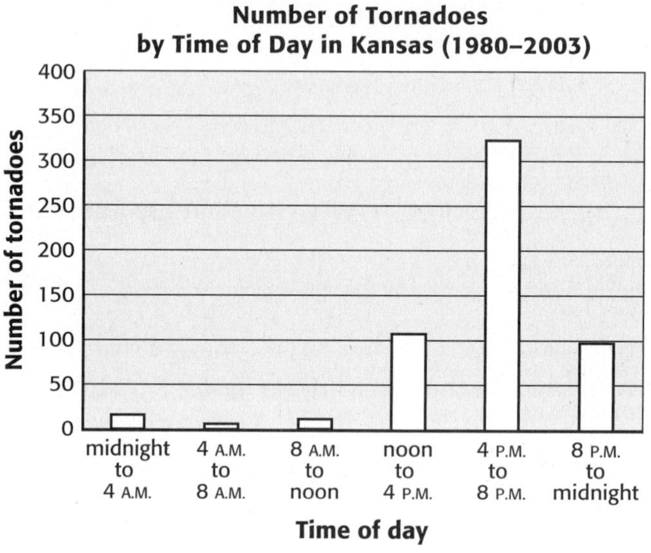

18. Evaluating During which time of day did the least tornadoes occur?

____

19. Concluding Would Kansas students be more likely to experience a tornado while they are at school or while they are at home? Explain your answer.

____

____

____

____

____

WRITING SKILLS

20. Communicating Concepts Write a short essay that explains how pressure, heat, air movement, and humidity result in changes in weather.

CRITICAL THINKING

21. Concept Mapping Use the following terms to create a concept map: *condensation, humidity, water cycle, dew point, precipitation, front, air masses, cyclone, lightning, tornado, thunder,* and *weather.*

22. Predicting Consequences How might the sun's cycle affect climate changes?

23. Making Inferences If both the air temperature and the amount of water vapor in the air change, is it possible for the relative humidity to stay the same? Explain your answer.

24. Evaluating Conclusions Explain why the climate on the eastern side of the Sierra Nevada differs drastically from the climate on the western side.

25. Identifying Relationships Explain the relationship between the tilt of Earth's axis and seasonal changes at different latitudes.

26. Applying Concepts Explain how convection currents affect wind patterns.

27. Predicting Consequences How would global climate be affected if Earth were not tilted on its axis? Explain your reasoning.

28. Predicting Consequences How would the water cycle be affected if the concentration of CO_2 in the atmosphere increased drastically?

29. Applying Concepts How can human activity affect the global climate?

INTERPRETING GRAPHICS

Use the map below to answer the next two questions.

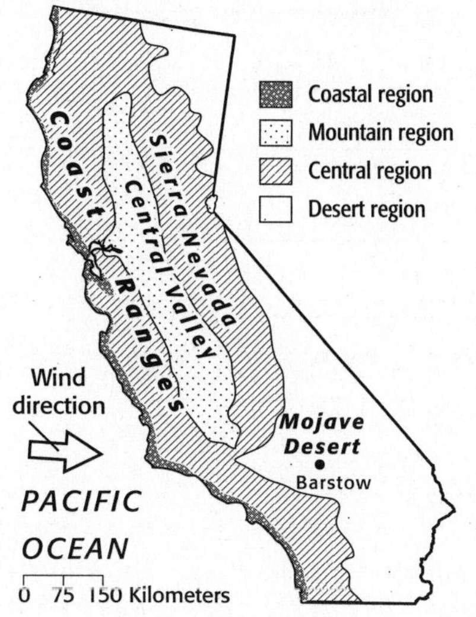

30. Evaluating Data Based on the map, identify two factors that influence the climates of California.

____

____

____

____

31. Analyzing Processes What major factor influences the amount of annual precipitation in the city of Barstow?

____

____

____

____

MATH SKILLS

32. Using Equations The temperature is 47°F. Using the equation °C = 5/9 × (°F − 32), find the temperature in degrees Celsius. Show your work below.

CHALLENGE

33. Predicting Consequences Describe how living things might be affected if global temperatures were, on the average, 5°C warmer. Over a long period of time, how might living things adapt to this change in temperature?

Assessment

Chapter Pretest

Teacher Notes and Answer Key

The Pretest questions are designed to help you determine the prior knowledge of your students. Some questions test whether students have mastered the background knowledge they need to understand the content you are about to teach. Other questions test your students' prior knowledge of the content you are about to teach. Use the Pretest with the Test Doctors and diagnostic teaching tips in these notes pages to help you tailor your instruction to your students' specific needs.

QUESTION NUMBER	CORRECT ANSWER	STANDARD
1	*C*	6.3.c
2	*C*	6.3.d
3	*B*	6.4.b
4	*D*	6.4.e
5	*C*	6.6.a
6	*A*	6.2.d
7	*D*	6.4.a
8	*B*	6.4.b
9	*B*	6.4.e
10	*D*	6.6.a

TEST DOCTOR

The following Pretest questions have been diagnosed by the Test Doctor. Find out what might be causing your students' "ailing" answers. Each Test Doctor is followed by a diagnostic teaching tip to help you address students' learning needs.

Question 1 *asks students to choose the statement about conduction and convection that is not true.*

A Incorrect. Heat flows in solids by conduction. There is direct physical contact between particles.
B Incorrect. Heat flows in fluids by convection. There is heat transfer during the circulation of a fluid.
C Correct. Heat does not flow through space by radiation.
D Incorrect. Heat flows in fluids by conduction.

Diagnostic Teaching Tip: Students who have difficulty answering this question should benefit from a review of conduction and convection. Use boiling water to illustrate convection and start a discussion. Have students touch a hot water bottle to illustrate conduction and start a discussion.

Question 2 *asks students to define radiation.*

A Incorrect. This is a definition of energy transfer by conduction.
B Incorrect. This is wrong because energy transfers by convection and conduction involve Earth's surface.
C Correct. Radiation is the transfer of energy as waves through space.

D **Incorrect.** This is a definition of energy transfer by convection.

Diagnostic Teaching Tip: Students who answer this question incorrectly should benefit from a review of radiation, conduction, and convection. Ask small groups of students to look up the word *radiation* in the dictionary. Ask them to copy the definition that relates most closely to the transfer of energy between the sun and Earth.

Question 3 *asks students what is true of solar energy as it radiates toward Earth's surface.*

A **Incorrect.** The upper atmosphere absorbs other forms of radiation—it absorbs almost all the radiation that has wavelengths shorter than visible light. But almost all visible light gets through.
B **Correct.** Most of the radiation that reaches Earth's surface is visible light.
C **Incorrect.** Ultraviolet rays are absorbed in the stratosphere.
D **Incorrect.** Most infrared radiation is absorbed by gases in the troposphere before it ever reaches Earth's surface.

Diagnostic Teaching Tip: Students who have difficulty answering this question correctly might benefit from a review of how Earth's atmosphere affects solar radiation. To start a discussion, ask students if a window shade that is pulled down blocks out all solar radiation. Explain that Earth's atmosphere filters out most of the ultraviolet rays, X rays, and gamma rays, but most of the visible light gets through.

Question 4 *asks students what happens when air from a high-pressure area flows toward a low-pressure area.*

A **Incorrect.** The air from a high-pressure area is cold and dense. It is doing the pushing, not getting pushed.
B **Incorrect.** This is not what happens when air from a high-pressure area flows toward a low-pressure area.
C **Incorrect.** The low-pressure area is already warm and less dense.
D **Correct.** The movement of air as it pushes the warm, less-dense air of the low-pressure area is wind.

Diagnostic Teaching Tip: Students who have trouble answering this question correctly should benefit from a review of air movement and wind. Open an outside door if it's cold outside, or remind students of what happens when they open a refrigerator door. Ask students about the rush of air. Use this to start a discussion of how wind is formed.

Question 5 *asks students to choose the answer that is not a cause of an increase in average global temperatures.*

A **Incorrect.** The burning of fossil fuels may cause an increase in average global temperatures.
B **Incorrect.** Greenhouse gases may cause an increase in average global temperatures because the gases absorb more heat.

C Correct. An increase in winds itself would not cause an increase in average global temperatures.

D Incorrect. An increased absorption of solar energy may cause an increase in average global temperatures.

Diagnostic Teaching Tip: Students who have difficulty answering this question correctly might benefit from a discussion about rising global temperatures. Conduct a step-by-step analysis of each response, and discuss why or why not each could contribute to an increase in average global temperatures.

Question 6 *asks students to identify the way that hurricanes cause the greatest changes to human and wildlife habitats.*

A Correct. The most damage caused by hurricanes comes from flooding caused by storm surges and heavy rains.

B Incorrect. Fires do not cause the greatest changes to human and wildlife habitats from hurricanes.

C Incorrect. Mud does not cause the greatest change to human and wildlife habitats.

D Incorrect. Landslides may occur as a result of hurricanes, but they do not cause the greatest changes to human and wildlife habitats.

Diagnostic Teaching Tip: Students who have difficulty with this question should discuss the effects of severe weather. Have students research Hurricane Rita or Hurricane Katrina and write a short report on the damage caused by the hurricane. Be sure to emphasize Section 2, "Fronts and Weather," in Chapter 15, "Weather and Climate." Students must know that floods change human and wildlife habitats in order to master standard 6.2.d.

Question 7 *asks students how the sun provides energy for Earth's water cycle.*

A Incorrect. Heat energy from the sun doesn't cause condensation, which is a process caused by cooling.

B Incorrect. Heat energy from the sun doesn't cause precipitation, which follows cooling and condensation.

C Incorrect. Runoff usually follows precipitation, which follows cooling.

D Correct. The heat energy from the sun causes liquid water to evaporate and form water vapor. The water cycle continues from there.

Diagnostic Teaching Tip: Students who have difficulty answering this question should discuss the water cycle and evaporation. Ask students what will happen to the contents of a glass of water over 24 hours, and start a discussion of evaporation. Be sure to emphasize Section 1, "Water in the Air," in Chapter 15, "Weather and Climate." Students must know that the sun is the major source of energy that powers the water cycle in order to master standard 6.4.a.

Question 8 *asks students why Earth's poles are colder than the equator.*

A Incorrect. The sun's radiation strikes the equator at a greater angle than the poles, and the solar energy is more concentrated at the equator.

B Correct. The sun's radiation strikes the poles at a lesser angle than the equator, and the solar energy is less concentrated at the poles.

C Incorrect. The sun's radiation strikes the poles at a lesser angle than the equator, and the solar energy is less concentrated at the poles.

D Incorrect. It is true that the sun's radiation strikes the equator at a greater angle than the poles, but the solar energy is more concentrated at the equator.

Diagnostic Teaching Tip: Students who have difficulty with this question should view a demonstration of solar energy and latitude. Use a globe and a light source to show the angles at which light hits the equator and the poles. Ask students where the light is more concentrated and why. Be sure to emphasize Section 3, "What Is Climate?," in Chapter 15, "Weather and Climate." Students must know that solar energy reaches Earth through radiation in order to master standard 6.4.b.

Question 9 *asks students what amount of Earth's atmosphere is water vapor.*

A Incorrect. The student may be thinking of liquid water.

B Correct. Water vapor makes up between 1% and 4% of Earth's atmosphere.

C Incorrect. The student may be thinking of liquid water.

D Incorrect. This answer reveals a lack of understanding of humidity or water vapor.

Diagnostic Teaching Tip: Students who have difficulty answering this question correctly should benefit from an introduction to humidity. Have students research what percentage of Earth is composed of water and what percentage of Earth's atmosphere is water vapor. Be sure to emphasize Section 1, "Water in the Air," in Chapter 15, "Weather and Climate." Students must know that differences in humidity result in changes of weather in order to master standard 6.4.e.

Question 10 *asks students to identify a consequence of using fossil fuels as an energy source.*

A Incorrect. The ozone layer is a naturally occurring phenomenon.

B Incorrect. The greenhouse effect occurs naturally; however, the use of fossil fuels has contributed to global warming through the greenhouse effect.

C Incorrect. Although burning forests contributes carbon dioxide to the atmosphere, it is not a consequence of using fossil fuels as an energy source.

D Correct. One of the factors that leads to global warming is increased carbon dioxide in the atmosphere as a result of using fossil fuels as an energy source.

Diagnostic Teaching Tip: Students who have difficulty answering this question correctly should benefit from a discussion of global warming and the use of fossil fuels. Ask students to discuss what they've learned about global warming from the news. Be sure to emphasize Section 4, "Changes in Climate," in Chapter 15, "Weather and Climate." Students must understand the consequences of using fossil fuels in order to master standard 6.6.a.

Name ______________________ Class ______________ Date ______________

Assessment

Chapter Pretest

______ **1.** Which of the following statements is NOT true?

A Heat flows in solids by conduction.
B Heat flows in fluids by convection.
C Heat flows through space by radiation.
D Heat flows in fluids by conduction.

______ **2.** What is radiation?

A the transfer of energy by direct physical contact
B any transfer of energy involving Earth's surface
C the transfer of energy as waves through space
D any transfer of energy by the circulation of fluids

______ **3.** What is true of solar energy as it radiates toward Earth's surface?

A The upper atmosphere absorbs most of the visible light.
B Most of the radiation that reaches Earth's surface is visible light.
C Most of the radiation that reaches Earth's surface is ultraviolet rays.
D The troposphere absorbs very little infrared radiation.

______ **4.** What happens when air from a high-pressure area flows toward a low-pressure area?

A The air from the low-pressure area pushes the air from the high-pressure area, and this movement of air causes ocean currents.
B Heat energy is transferred through radiation.
C The low-pressure area becomes warm and less dense.
D The air from a high-pressure area pushes the warm, less-dense air, and this movement of air is wind.

______ **5.** Which of the following would NOT cause an increase in average global temperatures?

A the burning of fossil fuels
B an increase in the amount of greenhouse gases
C an increase in winds
D an increased absorption of solar energy

______ **6.** In what way do hurricanes cause the greatest changes to human and wildlife habitats?

A flooding
B fires
C mud
D landslides

______ **7.** How does the sun provide energy for Earth's water cycle?
A Solar energy heats Earth's surface, causing condensation, which is water vapor changing into liquid water.
B Solar energy heats Earth's surface, causing precipitation, which is water falling as rain, snow, or hail.
C Solar energy heats Earth's surface, causing runoff, which is water flowing across land and collecting in rivers and streams.
D Solar energy heats Earth's surface, causing evaporation, which is liquid water changing into water vapor.

______ **8.** Why are Earth's poles colder than the equator?
A The sun's radiation strikes the equator at a lesser angle than the poles, and the solar energy is less concentrated at the equator.
B The sun's radiation strikes the poles at a lesser angle than the equator, and the solar energy is less concentrated at the poles.
C The sun's radiation strikes the poles at a greater angle than the equator, and the solar energy is more concentrated at the poles.
D The sun's radiation strikes the equator at a greater angle than the poles, and the solar energy is less concentrated at the equator.

______ **9.** The humidity in Earth's atmosphere has a direct effect on weather. What amount of Earth's atmosphere is water vapor?
A 70%
B between 1% and 4%
C between 50% and 55%
D 20%

______ **10.** Which of the following is a consequence of using fossil fuels as an energy source?
A the ozone layer
B the greenhouse effect
C burning forests to clear land for farming
D global warming

Name ______________________ Class ______________ Date ____________

Assessment

Section Quiz

Section: Water in the Air

Match the correct definition with the correct term. Write the letter in the space provided.

_____ **1.** the ratio of the amount of water vapor in the air to the amount of water vapor needed to reach saturation

_____ **2.** the change of state from a gas to a liquid

_____ **3.** water droplets that form on things near the ground when air cools to below the dew point

_____ **4.** the amount of water vapor in the air

_____ **5.** any form of water that falls to Earth's surface from the clouds

a. precipitation
b. condensation
c. humidity
d. relative humidity
e. dew

Write the letter of the correct answer in the space provided.

_____ **6.** The short-term state of the atmosphere is called
a. climate.
b. weather.
c. water cycle.
d. dew point.

_____ **7.** What happens when the rate of evaporation equals the rate of condensation?
a. Precipitation occurs.
b. The dew point is reached.
c. The humidity decreases.
d. Clouds form.

_____ **8.** The most common form of precipitation is
a. sleet.
b. hail.
c. rain.
d. snow.

_____ **9.** The sun's energy causes water to change states through
a. relative humidity.
b. ice crystals.
c. weather.
d. the water cycle.

Name ______________________ Class ______________ Date ______________

Assessment

Section Quiz

Section: Fronts and Weather

Match the correct definition with the correct term. Write the letter in the space provided.

______ **1.** an electric discharge that takes place between two oppositely charged surfaces

______ **2.** an area in the atmosphere that has lower pressure than the surrounding areas, with winds that spiral toward the center

______ **3.** the sound caused by the rapid expansion of air along an electrical strike

______ **4.** a rotating column of air that has very high wind speeds and that may be visible as a funnel-shaped cloud

a. thunder
b. lightning
c. tornado
d. cyclone

Write the letter of the correct answer in the space provided.

______ **5.** Changes in weather are caused by the interaction of
a. cyclones.
b. anticyclones.
c. fronts.
d. air masses.

______ **6.** How does a warm front form?
a. Warm air becomes caught between cold air masses.
b. Two air masses meet and stay separated.
c. Warm air moves over cold air and replaces it.
d. Cold air moves under warm air and pushes it up.

______ **7.** What is an area in which two or more air masses meet?
a. front
b. air mass
c. tornado
d. storm surge

______ **8.** Which of the following statements describes an anticyclone?
a. It is an area of low pressure.
b. It is an area of high pressure.
c. It has air masses that meet and rise.
d. It moves in the direction of Earth's rotation.

______ **9.** A rise in sea level during a storm that causes property damage and endangers lives is a(n)
a. air mass.
b. tornado.
c. storm surge.
d. hurricane.

Name ______________________ Class ______________ Date ____________

Assessment

Section Quiz

Section: What Is Climate?

Match the correct description with the correct term. Write the letter in the space provided.

_____ **1.** the height of a surface landform above sea level

_____ **2.** a horizontal movement of ocean water that is caused by wind

_____ **3.** the average weather conditions over a long period of time

_____ **4.** the distance north or south from the equator

a. surface current
b. latitude
c. elevation
d. climate

Write the letter of the correct answer in the space provided.

_____ **5.** Which of the following is the cause of the change of seasons?
a. the process called rain-shadow effect
b. the sizes and shapes of land-surface features
c. the tilt of Earth's axis
d. the rotation of Earth

_____ **6.** Which of the following statements explains the rain-shadow effect?
a. Mountains force air to rise; air cools and releases moisture as it rises.
b. The atmosphere gets denser as elevation increases, causing snow to fall.
c. Temperatures are higher on one side of a mountain than on the other.
d. Wind patterns cause precipitation.

_____ **7.** What helps keep temperatures along the West Coast cooler than inland temperatures all year long?
a. solar energy
b. rain-shadow effect
c. topography
d. surface currents

_____ **8.** Which of the following statements is NOT true about winds?
a. Winds carry evaporated water away from the ocean surface.
b. Winds carry solar energy to and from different locations.
c. Winds move in unpredictable patterns across Earth's surface.
d. Winds blow from areas of high pressure to areas of low pressure.

_____ **9.** Earth's three major climate zones are
a. polar, tropical, and rain forest.
b. tropical, temperate, and polar.
c. tundra, temperate, and tropical.
d. polar, savanna, and rain forest.

Name ______________________ Class ______________ Date ____________

Assessment

Section Quiz

Section: Changes in Climate

Match the correct description with the correct term. Write the letter in the space provided.

_____ **1.** when water vapor, carbon dioxide, and other gases absorb and reradiate thermal energy

_____ **2.** a long period of climate cooling during which the continents are glaciated repeatedly

_____ **3.** a gradual increase in the average global temperature

a. ice age
b. greenhouse effect
c. global warming

Write the letter of the correct answer in the space provided.

_____ **4.** The Milankovitch theory states that
a. ice ages are caused by volcanic eruptions.
b. continental drift causes ice ages.
c. changes in the Earth's orbit cause ice ages.
d. Earth's orbit never changes.

_____ **5.** How would an asteroid most likely change Earth's climate?
a. Debris from an asteroid hitting Earth could block sunlight.
b. The asteroid would block the sun during its orbit, chilling Earth.
c. The asteroid would change Earth's orbit, causing an ice age.
d. If the asteroid fell in the ocean, it would make the sea level rise.

_____ **6.** Which of the following is NOT a cause of an increase in carbon dioxide in the atmosphere?
a. burning fuels for transportation
b. clearing forests for farming
c. burning fuels for industry
d. planting trees

_____ **7.** During glacial periods,
a. large sheets of ice get smaller.
b. large sheets of ice advance.
c. large sheets of ice retreat.
d. large sheets of ice melt.

Name ______________________ Class ______________ Date ____________

Assessment

Chapter Test A

Weather and Climate

MULTIPLE CHOICE

Write the letter of the correct answer in the space provided.

______ **1.** What is the water cycle?
- **a.** air masses meeting
- **b.** air pressure sinking and then rising
- **c.** water droplets forming on surfaces
- **d.** water moving between the atmosphere, the land, and the oceans

______ **2.** What causes changes in weather?
- **a.** Air masses interact.
- **b.** The air gets more humid.
- **c.** Water evaporates.
- **d.** Clouds form.

______ **3.** What kind of air pressure is in a cyclone?
- **a.** very dense
- **b.** higher than surrounding areas
- **c.** sinking and then rising
- **d.** lower than surrounding areas

______ **4.** What causes lightning?
- **a.** thunder
- **b.** an electric discharge
- **c.** rising warm air
- **d.** air masses meeting

______ **5.** Which of the following describes relative humidity?
- **a.** a measure of how close air is to the dew point
- **b.** the condition of the atmosphere at a certain time
- **c.** the movement of air masses
- **d.** a gradual increase in Earth's temperatures

______ **6.** Which of the following helps to keep California's temperatures moderate?
- **a.** the rain-shadow effect
- **b.** the sun
- **c.** the Great Lakes
- **d.** the ocean

______ **7.** Where does a cold front form?
a. where cold air moves under warm air
b. where warm air moves over cold air
c. where two air masses remain separated
d. where warm air masses move quickly

______ **8.** When temperatures fall below 0°C, what forms in a cloud?
a. ice crystals
b. gases
c. water droplets
d. dew

______ **9.** What is a cloud made of?
a. gases
b. water droplets
c. snow
d. warm air

______ **10.** Which of the following is a rapidly spinning column of air that touches the ground?
a. air mass
b. thunder
c. tornado
d. hurricane

______ **11.** Which of the following weather conditions causes the most deaths?
a. thunderstorm
b. flash flood
c. cyclone
d. hail

MATCHING

Match the correct description with the correct term. Write the letter in the space provided.

______ **12.** the temperature at which air is saturated

______ **13.** average weather in an area for a long time

______ **14.** distance from the equator

______ **15.** the condition of the atmosphere at a certain time and place

a. climate
b. weather
c. dew point
d. latitude

Match the correct description with the correct term. Write the letter in the space provided.

_____ **16.** the sound caused by air rapidly expanding along an electrical strike

_____ **17.** the amount of water vapor in the air

_____ **18.** streamlike movement of water on the top of the ocean's surface

_____ **19.** water that falls to Earth's surface

a. precipitation

b. surface current

c. humidity

d. thunder

FILL-IN-THE-BLANK

Use the terms from the following list to complete the sentences below.

condensation greenhouse effect global warming

20. When a gas changes to a liquid, it is called ______________________.

21. Earth's natural heating process is called ______________________.

22. When the global temperature rises bit by bit it is called

______________________.

Use the terms from the following list to complete the sentences below.

ice age elevation front

23. The height of surface landforms above sea level is the

______________________.

24. Ice forms in high latitudes and moves toward lower latitudes

during a(n) ______________________.

25. The boundary between different air masses is called

______________________.

Assessment

Chapter Test B

Weather and Climate

MATCHING

Match the correct description with the correct term. Write the letter in the space provided.

______	**1.** the amount of water vapor in the air	**a.** dew point
______	**2.** the sound caused by the release of energy	**b.** thunder
______	**3.** the temperature at which the rate of evaporation equals the rate of condensation	**c.** humidity
______	**4.** the process in which water vapor turns to liquid	**d.** front
______	**5.** an area of low pressure where air masses meet and rise	**e.** condensation
______	**6.** an area in which two kinds of air masses meet	**f.** cyclone

MULTIPLE CHOICE

Write the letter of the correct answer in the space provided.

______ **7.** What kind of weather does a stationary front bring?
- **a.** drizzly rain followed by clear weather
- **b.** severe storms
- **c.** many days of cloudy, wet weather
- **d.** cold, dry weather

______ **8.** Finding a high place to wait is a safety measure during a(n)
- **a.** thunderstorm.
- **b.** tornado.
- **c.** cyclone.
- **d.** flash flood.

______ **9.** When it touches the ground, a funnel cloud becomes a(n)
- **a.** hurricane.
- **b.** thunderstorm.
- **c.** anticyclone.
- **d.** tornado.

______ **10.** Lightning is an electric discharge between a positively charged area and
- **a.** a rising air mass.
- **b.** a stationary front.
- **c.** another positively charged area.
- **d.** a negatively charged area.

______ **11.** Why does the equator experience high temperatures year round?
a. It has a high latitude.
b. It has no large bodies of water.
c. The sun's rays hit it at a lesser angle.
d. The sun's rays hit it directly.

MATCHING

Match the correct definition with the correct term. Write the letter in the space provided.

______ **12.** the short-term state of the atmosphere

______ **13.** the average weather condition in an area over a long period of time

a. climate
b. weather

MULTIPLE CHOICE

Write the letter of the correct answer in the space provided.

______ **14.** Global warming may be caused by
a. changes in weather patterns.
b. an increase in carbon dioxide concentrations.
c. a decrease in carbon dioxide concentrations.
d. the tilt of Earth's axis.

______ **15.** Changes in weather are the interaction of
a. clouds.
b. tornadoes.
c. storm surges.
d. air masses.

______ **16.** What do scientists use to express the amount of water vapor in the air?
a. relative humidity
b. vapor pressure
c. elevation
d. dew point

______ **17.** When droplets in a cloud reach a certain size, they
a. form a cold front.
b. fall as precipitation.
c. cause an electric discharge.
d. change the climate of an area.

______ **18.** Which of the following is NOT true of an ice age?
a. Ice forms in high latitudes and moves toward lower latitudes.
b. There are periods of cold and periods of warmth.
c. There have been few major ice ages.
d. Ice sheets advance and get bigger.

______ **19.** Earth's natural heating process is called
a. the greenhouse effect.
b. global warming.
c. an ice age.
d. the Milankovitch theory.

______ **20.** Which of the following decreases as elevation increases?
a. latitude
b. clouds
c. precipitation
d. temperature

______ **21.** As surface currents move,
a. they release heat quickly.
b. they influence the amount of solar energy an area receives.
c. they carry warm or cool water to different locations.
d. they bring warm temperatures to the West Coast.

______ **22.** The distance north or south from the equator is called
a. the rain-shadow effect.
b. elevation.
c. topography.
d. latitude.

MATCHING

Match the labels to the map. Write the letters in the spaces provided.

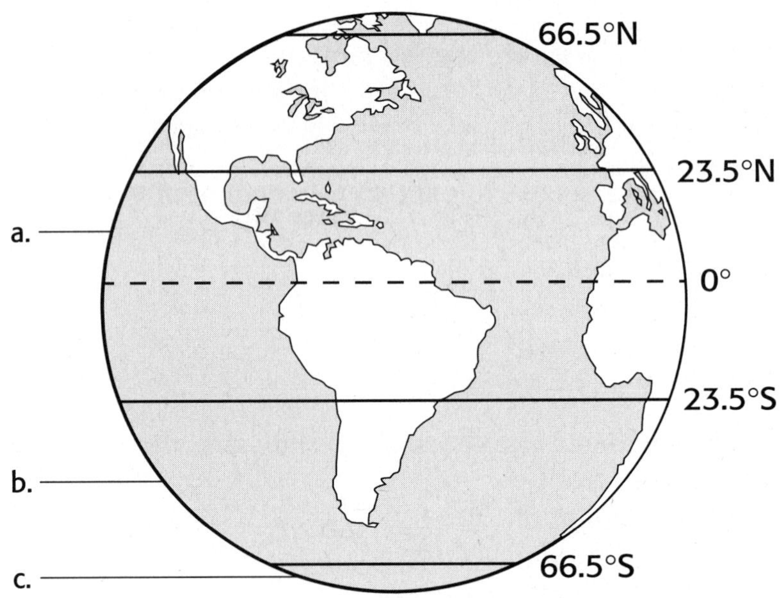

______ **23.** temperate

______ **24.** polar

______ **25.** tropical

Name ______________________ Class ______________ Date ____________

Assessment

Chapter Test C

Weather and Climate

USING KEY TERMS

Use the terms from the following list to complete the sentences below. Each term may be used only once. Some terms may not be used.

elevation	latitudes	greenhouse effect
air masses	relative humidity	condensation
precipitation	weather	humidity

1. A measure of how close the air is to dew point is ______________________.

2. The day-to-day change in temperature and precipitation makes up an area's ______________________.

3. Gases in the atmosphere absorb and reradiate thermal energy, causing the ______________________.

4. People use coasters when setting cold drinks on furniture to protect the surface from ______________________.

5. The curve of Earth affects the amount of direct solar energy at different ______________________.

6. Hail is a less common form of ______________________.

UNDERSTANDING KEY IDEAS

Write the letter of the correct answer in the space provided.

______ **7.** Seasons are caused by
a. ocean currents.
b. the greenhouse effect.
c. the rain-shadow effect.
d. the tilt of Earth's axis.

______ **8.** Humidity is
a. the amount of water vapor in the air.
b. the temperature below dew point.
c. when a gas becomes a liquid.
d. the continuous movement of water.

______ **9.** Streamlike movements of water that have a large affect on an area's climate are
a. water vapor.
b. dew.
c. surface currents.
d. storm surges.

______ **10.** At higher elevations,
- **a.** there is no rain-shadow effect.
- **b.** the temperature of the air is lower.
- **c.** the dew point is higher.
- **d.** the temperature of the air is higher.

______ **11.** Temperature and amount of precipitation are used to describe
- **a.** latitude.
- **b.** surface currents.
- **c.** clouds.
- **d.** climate.

______ **12.** When air is nearly saturated and temperature drops, what is reached?
- **a.** dew point
- **b.** condensation
- **c.** precipitation
- **d.** humidity

______ **13.** Global warming is caused in part by
- **a.** increases in carbon dioxide concentrations.
- **b.** volcanic eruptions.
- **c.** glacial and interglacial periods.
- **d.** the tilt of Earth's axis.

14. Explain how lightning and thunder form.

____

____

____

____

____

____

15. Explain what happens during a storm surge.

____

____

____

16. How does a cloud form?

____

____

____

CRITICAL THINKING

17. Most hurricanes that form in the North Atlantic Ocean occur from June to November, with most hurricanes occurring in September. What facts about hurricane formation help explain this?

18. What happens during an ice age?

19. Briefly describe three causes of climate change on Earth.

CONCEPT MAPPING

20. Use the following terms to complete the concept map below:

cyclone hurricane tornado
front air masses

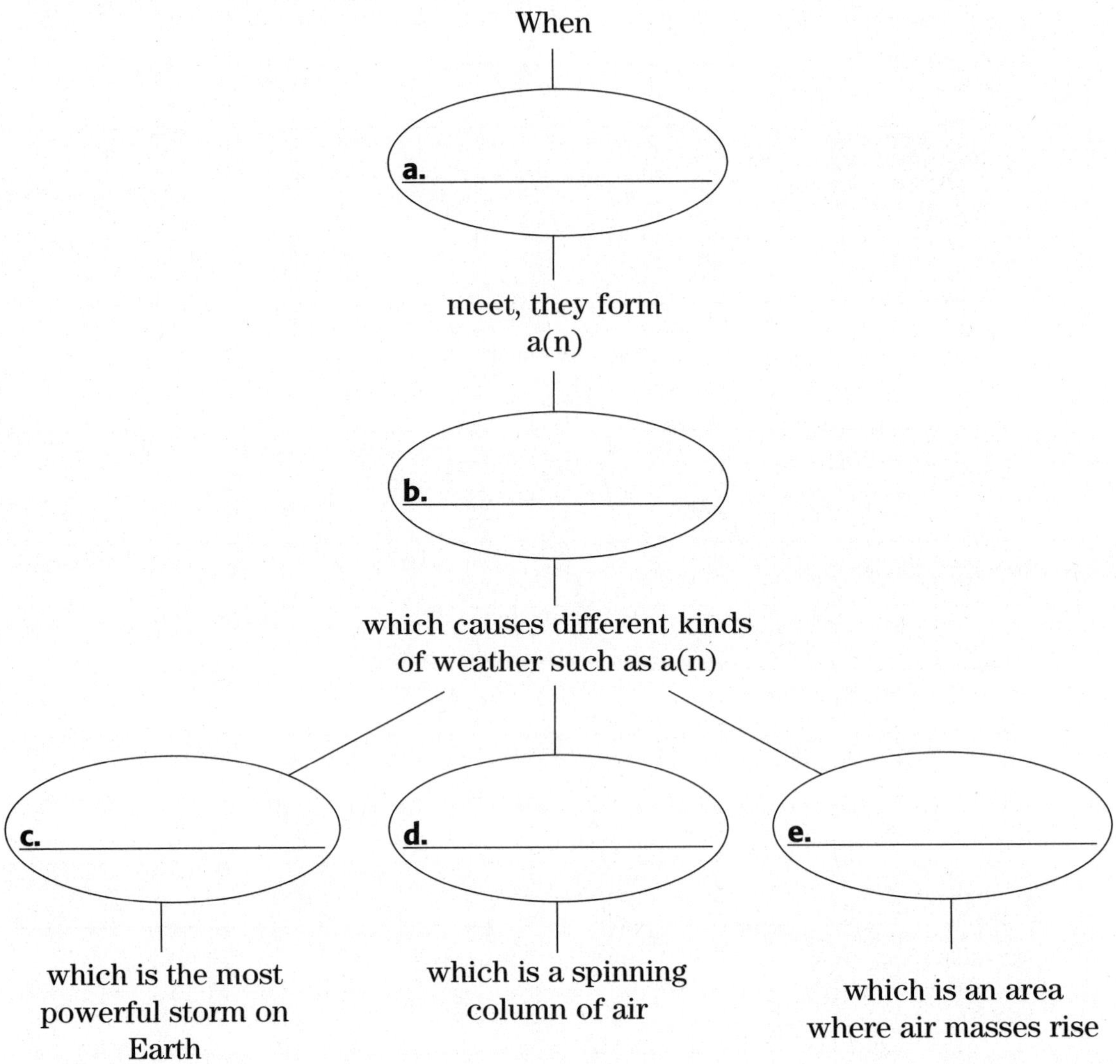

Assessment

Performance-Based Assessment

Teacher Notes

PURPOSE

Students will model the ocean and observe how currents flow.

CLASSROOM TESTED & APPROVED

Bert Sherwood
Socorro Middle School
El Paso, Texas

TIME REQUIRED

35 minutes. Students will need 15 minutes at the activity station and 20 minutes to answer the questions.

RATING

Easy ← 1 2 3 4 → Hard

Teacher Prep–2
Student Set-Up–1
Concept Level–2
Clean Up–1

ADVANCE PREPARATION

Equip each activity station with the necessary materials.

SAFETY CAUTION

Water is a slipping hazard. Wipe up spills immediately.

TEACHING STRATEGIES

This activity works best in groups of 3–4 students. Before the activity review the definition of *surface currents* and discuss what students have read about large bodies of water and their effect on climate.

Some students may require additional guidance in the Analysis section. Ask students what effect the warm water at the top of the ocean has on the surrounding air, and what effect the warm air has on the climate of nearby land areas.

Evaluation Strategies

Use the following rubric to help evaluate student performance.

Rubric for Assessment

Possible points	Lab technique (50 points possible)
50–25	Successfully completes activity; safe and careful handling of materials and equipment; superior lab skills; colored water is clearly separate
24–1	Attempts to complete activity; apparent lack of skill; tasks yield inadequate results; lack of effort
	Comprehesion of concepts (50 points possible)
50–25	Answers show depth of understanding
24–1	Poor understanding of ocean currents and their effect on climate

Name ______________________ Class ______________ Date ____________

Assessment

MODEL-MAKING

Performance-Based Assessment

OBJECTIVE

You've read about ocean currents and their effect on climates. Now you will create currents in an aquarium and discuss how the behavior of water affects currents in the ocean.

KNOW THE SCORE!

As you work through the activity, keep in mind that you will be earning a grade for the following:

- your lab technique (50%)
- your understanding of ocean currents (50%)

MATERIALS AND EQUIPMENT

- food coloring, blue
- plate, plastic or metal, to fit inside the box
- "shoebox," 4 L clear plastic
- water, warm and cold

SAFETY INFORMATION

- Water is a slipping hazard. Wipe up spills immediately.

Using Scientific Methods

ASK A QUESTION

How does the behavior of water affect currents in the ocean?

FORM A HYPOTHESIS

1. What do you think happens to cold water when it is poured into a body of warm water?

____

____

____

____

____

____

____

TEST THE HYPOTHESIS

2. Carefully pour about 3 L of warm water into the box.

3. In a separate container, add 20 drops of food coloring to about 500 mL of very cold water.

4. Place the plate in the box near one of the sides to form a slope to the bottom.

5. Slowly and carefully pour the colored water over the plate and into the aquarium.

ANALYZE THE RESULTS

6. Describe what you observed when you poured the colored water into the aquarium.

____

____

DRAW CONCLUSIONS

7. Why is the phenomenon you observed important to regions near large bodies of water?

____

____

____

____

BIG IDEA QUESTION

8. How do ocean currents affect California's climate? Explain your answer.

____

____

____

____

____

____

____

Assessment

Standards Assessment

Teacher Notes and Answer Key

To provide practice under more realistic testing conditions, give students 20 min to answer all of the questions in this assessment.

QUESTION NUMBER	CORRECT ANSWER	STANDARD
1	*C*	6.3.c (supporting)
2	*B*	6.4.a (supporting)
3	*C*	6.4.d (supporting)
4	*A*	6.7 (supporting)
5	*B*	6.4.a (exceeding)
6	*A*	6.6.a (supporting)
7	*C*	6.2.d (mastering)
8	*D*	6.4.b (supporting)
9	*B*	6.4.e (mastering)
10	*C*	6.4.e (exceeding)
11	*B*	5.4.c (mastering)
12	*C*	5.4.d (mastering)
13	*C*	5.4.e (mastering)
14	*D*	6.3.a (mastering)

TEST DOCTOR

The following Standards Assessment questions have been diagnosed by the Test Doctor. Find out what might be causing your students' "ailing" answers. Each Test Doctor is followed by a diagnostic teaching tip to help you address students' learning needs.

Question 1 *asks students to define the word* involves *in context.*

A Incorrect. Convection does not take part in the flow of matter.
B Incorrect. *Involves* does not mean "is a part of."
C Correct. Convection involves, or includes, the flow of matter.
D Incorrect. Convection does not need the flow of matter.

Diagnostic Teaching Tip: Students who have difficulty with this question might benefit from reviewing the steps involved in the process of convection. Review the behavior of air molecules when they are heated. Have students draw a sequential diagram of the process at a molecular level.

Question 2 *asks students to recognize the definition of the word* cycle.

A Incorrect. Energy is not a repeating series of changes.
B Correct. A cycle consists of a repeating series of changes.
C Incorrect. Erosion may be a part of a repeating series of changes, but it is only one specific part and not the best answer.
D Incorrect. A phenomenon is not necessarily repeated.

Diagnostic Teaching Tip: Students who have difficulty with this question might benefit from a deeper understanding of the meaning of the word *cycle*. Begin with the word *bicycle* and ask students to speculate on what the two parts of the word mean. Ask students to guess on the basis of your discussion what shape a cycle is. Invite them to name some phenomena they have learned about in science that occur in cycles, such as the repetition of night and day, the phases of the moon, the water cycle, and the life cycle of organisms.

Question 3 *asks students to identify the correct definition of* distribute *in context.*

A **Incorrect.** To distribute is not to eliminate.
B **Incorrect.** *Distribute* is nearly the opposite of *focus*.
C **Correct.** *Distribute* means "to spread over an area."
D **Incorrect.** Something that is distributed is not necessarily strengthened.

Diagnostic Teaching Tip: Students who have difficulty answering this question correctly might benefit from writing a paragraph that uses *distribute*, as well as each of the other answer choices. Encourage students to write about convection, and then invite them to read their paragraphs to a partner.

Question 4 *asks students to identify the correct definition of* investigation.

A **Correct.** An investigation is a detailed search for answers.
B **Incorrect.** A series of actions directed toward an aim is not necessarily an investigation.
C **Incorrect.** "A request for information or for a reply" is the definition of question.
D **Incorrect.** An answer to a puzzle or question is a solution.

Diagnostic Teaching Tip: Students who have difficulty with this question might benefit from discussing how each answer choice plays a role in an investigation. Ask volunteers to explain how a process, question, and solution each might be part of an investigation.

Question 5 *asks students to demonstrate understanding of the water cycle.*

A **Incorrect.** Convection is not a step in the water cycle.
B **Correct.** Condensation follows evaporation and leads to precipitation.
C **Incorrect.** Reclamation is not a step in the water cycle.
D **Incorrect.** There is no step in the water cycle called reformation.

Diagnostic Teaching Tip: Students who struggle with this type of question might benefit from reviewing the steps in the water cycle. Divide students into groups of four, and assign each student one step of the water cycle as shown in the diagram. Have students go around the circle in their groups and describe the water cycle step by step.

Question 6 *asks students to demonstrate understanding of carbon dioxide's role in global warming.*

A Correct. Carbon dioxide absorbs the sun's heat as it is radiated back from Earth. In this way carbon dioxide has a similar result as the glass of a greenhouse as it traps heat energy, leading to warmer global temperatures.

B Incorrect. Carbon dioxide does not directly cause warm fronts that heat Earth.

C Incorrect. Carbon dioxide does not have "natural radiation."

D Incorrect. Carbon dioxide does not directly cause warm ocean currents.

Diagnostic Teaching Tip: Students who struggle with this question might benefit from learning why greenhouses can be so warm, even on a winter day. Explain that the glass permits solar radiation to enter and heat the interior of the greenhouse, but the glass prevents all of the heat from radiating back to the environment. Explain that carbon dioxide leads to a similar result in the atmosphere.

Question 7 *asks students to describe how volcanoes can cause climate change.*

A Incorrect. Dust and ash from volcanoes do not warm Earth.

B Incorrect. Volcanic lava does not affect Earth's climate.

C Correct. Dust and ash particles can cool the climate by blocking the sun's rays.

D Incorrect. Volcanoes do not change the climate by shifting tectonic plates.

Diagnostic Teaching Tip: Students who have difficulty answering this question correctly might benefit from deepening their understanding of the effects volcanic eruption can have on global climates. Invite students to research accounts of how the eruption of Mount St. Helens affected climate locally and globally. Invite students to share their findings.

Question 8 *asks students to demonstrate understanding of the sun's effect on global climates.*

A Incorrect. The North Pole's distance from the sun does not make the North Pole cooler than the equator.

B Incorrect. During the summer, days are longer at the North Pole than they are at the equator.

C Incorrect. The North Pole's climate is not a result of air currents.

D Correct. The sun's rays are less direct at the North Pole than at the equator because of the difference in the angle of the incoming solar radiation.

Diagnostic Teaching Tip: Students who have difficulty with this question might benefit from an experiment that shows how the sun's rays hit different parts of Earth. Have students use an orange and a flashlight or a globe and a desk lamp to represent Earth and the sun. Note that when the flashlight is pointed directly at the orange, the light at the top and bottom of the orange looks weaker and more diffused.

Question 9 *asks students to demonstrate understanding of the interaction between oceans and the atmosphere in the formation of hurricanes.*

A Incorrect. Hurricanes do not form over land.

B Correct. When thunderstorms meet over warm ocean water, hurricanes can form.

C Incorrect. Warm ocean water rather than cool water is ideal for hurricane formation.

D Incorrect. Hurricanes are not formed where warm and cold fronts meet.

Diagnostic Teaching Tip: Students who have difficulty answering this question correctly might benefit from investigating the conditions under which real hurricanes have formed. Have students do library and Internet research to find out where recent hurricanes originated. In class, discuss why those areas were likely places for hurricane formation.

Question 10 *asks students to interpret a graph of humidity over time.*

A Incorrect. At 2:00 P.M., the humidity rises to 100 percent. A cold front would not necessarily cause the humidity to rise.

B Incorrect. A warm front does not raise the humidity to 100 percent.

C Correct. Rain or fog is likely to occur when the humidity reaches 100 percent.

D Incorrect. If evaporation were taking place at 2 P.M., the humidity would increase as a result. But the chart indicates that the humidity falls sharply after 2 P.M.

Diagnostic Teaching Tip: Students who have difficulty with this question might benefit from reviewing how humidity factors into the water cycle. Have students working in pairs create a flip book that shows a humidity gauge whose levels change throughout the steps in the water cycle. Remind students that high humidity means that there is a large amount of water vapor in the air, which will eventually turn into precipitation.

Question 11 *asks students to identify what happens when warm and cold air meet.*

A Incorrect. This interaction does not lead to evaporation.

B Correct. When warm, humid air comes into contact with a cold air mass, the water in the warm, humid air condenses and creates precipitation.

C Incorrect. The meeting of warm, humid air and cold air is not enough to create a hurricane.

D Incorrect. Cold air pushes warm air upward, not vice versa.

Diagnostic Teaching Tip: Students who have difficulty answering this question correctly might benefit from discussing how the dew point changes when temperature changes. Note that as the dew point decreases, the humid air becomes more likely to condense. Help students create a graph that shows the relationship between these two factors.

Question 12 *asks students to demonstrate understanding that high-pressure areas move toward low-pressure areas.*

A Incorrect. In this scenario, the clouds will not move west.
B Incorrect. There is nothing in this scenario to suggest warm air will cause clouds to evaporate.
C Correct. The clouds will move east, because an area of high pressure flows toward an area of low pressure.
D Incorrect. This scenario is not likely to create a thunderstorm.

Diagnostic Teaching Tip: Students who struggle to answer this type of question might benefit by creating a visual map of the scenario as it is described. For additional review, collect several days' worth of weather maps from the newspaper or weather Web sites, and have students analyze in writing the movements of high- and low-pressure regions and how the weather behaved in predictable and unpredictable ways from one day to the next.

Question 13 *asks students to demonstrate understanding of the pressure exerted by Earth's atmosphere.*

A Incorrect. At a given point, the atmosphere exerts the same degree of pressure in all directions.
B Incorrect. Air pressure is lowest in upper areas of the atmosphere.
C Correct. Air pressure is greatest closest to Earth, so atmospheric pressure increases as altitude decreases.
D Incorrect. Air pressure is not equal at all levels of the atmosphere.

Diagnostic Teaching Tip: Students who have difficulty with this question might benefit from discussing gravity's effects on air molecules. Illustrate this concept by drawing a model of the atmosphere on the board that shows how gravity affects air molecules at sea level. Discuss whether gravity is stronger or weaker the farther the molecules move from Earth's surface. Then, have students diagram and label how gravity will affect the molecules below and above sea level.

Question 14 *asks students to identify radiation as the process by which the sun heats Earth.*

A Incorrect. Conduction involves heat passing through solids, not through space.
B Incorrect. The sun creates evaporation, but evaporation does not heat Earth.
C Incorrect. Convection takes place through fluids or gases, but not through space, which is a vacuum.
D Correct. The sun heats Earth by the process of radiation.

Diagnostic Teaching Tip: Students who have difficulty with this question might benefit from reviewing the processes of conduction, convection, and radiation. Have groups of three work together to create a poster showing everyday examples of each method of energy transfer.

Name ______________________ Class ______________ Date ____________

Assessment

Standards Assessment

REVIEWING ACADEMIC VOCABULARY

_____ **1.** In the sentence "Convection is a process that involves the flow of fluids," what does the word *involves* mean?

A takes part in
B is strengthened by
C to have as a part of
D needs

_____ **2.** Which of the following words means "a repeating series of changes"?

A energy
B cycle
C erosion
D phenomenon

_____ **3.** In the sentence "Convection currents distribute heat throughout the atmosphere," what does the word *distribute* mean?

A eliminate
B focus all attention on
C to spread over an area
D strengthen

_____ **4.** Which of the following words is the closest in meaning to the word *investigation*?

A a detailed search for answers
B a series of actions directed toward an aim
C a request for information or for a reply
D an answer to a puzzle or question

REVIEWING CONCEPTS

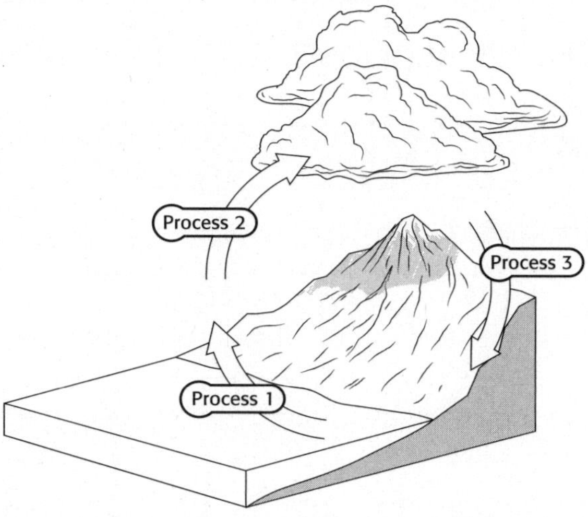

______ **5.** Which word best describes Process 2 in the diagram above?
A convection
B condensation
C reclamation
D reformation

______ **6.** Carbon dioxide in the atmosphere can lead to global warming. How can carbon dioxide cause this phenomenon?
A It absorbs heat and keeps heat in the atmosphere.
B It creates warm fronts that heat Earth.
C Its natural radiation heats Earth.
D It causes warm ocean currents that heat Earth.

______ **7.** How can volcanoes cause climate change?
A by warming Earth with a blanket of dust and ash particles
B by warming Earth with volcanic lava
C by blocking the sun's rays with dust and ash so that Earth cools
D by shifting tectonic plates

______ **8.** Why is the climate at the North Pole cooler than the climate near the equator?
A because the North Pole is farther from the sun
B because days last much longer at the equator
C because cold air currents make the North Pole cooler
D because the sun's rays hit the North Pole at an angle

______ **9.** Under which of the following conditions is a hurricane most likely to form?
A when high and low pressure zones meet over warm land
B when thunderstorms meet over warm ocean water
C when thunderstorms meet over cool ocean water
D when warm and cold fronts meet over warm water

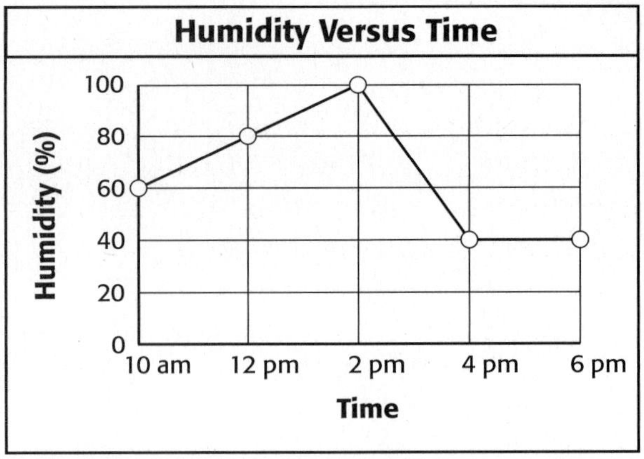

______ **10.** Which of the following events most likely occurred at 2:00 pm in the graph above?
A a cold front
B a warm front
C rain showers
D evaporation

REVIEWING PRIOR LEARNING

______ **11.** Which of the following is most likely to occur when warm, humid air comes into contact with a cold air mass?
A Water on the ground evaporates.
B Condensation and precipitation occur.
C A hurricane or tropical storm forms.
D The cold air mass is pushed upward.

______ **12.** Clouds are observed in a high-pressure area over California, and clear skies are observed in a low-pressure area directly to the east. Which of the following is most likely to occur?
A Wind will blow the clouds in a westerly direction.
B The warm air will cause the clouds to evaporate.
C The clouds will move east to the low-pressure area.
D A thunderstorm will occur between the two areas.

______ **13.** Which of the following statements about Earth's atmosphere is true?
A The atmosphere exerts greater downward than upward pressure.
B Pressure is highest in upper areas of the atmosphere.
C Atmospheric pressure increases as altitude decreases.
D Pressure is equal at all levels of the atmosphere.

______ **14.** By what process does the sun heat Earth?
A conduction
B evaporation
C convection
D radiation

Explore Activity

DATASHEET

The Meeting of Air Masses

Teacher Notes

This activity helps students understand what happens when two air masses meet (covers standard 6.4.e). Students should be able to distinguish the oil from the water when the two liquids are poured together. If not, try the experiment again using water that is colored with food coloring.

MATERIALS

For each group

- beakers (2)
- container, clear plastic, rectangular
- cooking oil, 500 mL
- water, 500 mL

SAFETY CAUTION

Remind students to review all safety cautions and icons before beginning this activity.

Name ______________________ Class ______________ Date ____________

Explore Activity

DATASHEET A

The Meeting of Air Masses

In this activity, you will model what happens when two air masses that have different temperature characteristics meet.

SAFETY INFORMATION

PROCEDURE

1. Pour **500 mL of water** into a **beaker.**
   - The water represents a dense, cold air mass.
   - Pour **500 mL of cooking oil** into a **second beaker**.
   - The cooking oil represents a less dense, warm air mass.
2. Predict what would happen to the two liquids if you tried to mix them.

   ____

   ____

3. From opposite ends of the container:
   - Pour the contents of both beakers into a **clear, plastic, rectangular container** at the same time
4. Observe what happens to the oil and water.

ANALYSIS

5. What happens when the two liquids meet?

   ____

   ____

   - Which liquid ends up on top?

   ____

6. Does the prediction that you made in step 2 match your results?

   ____

   ____

7. Based on the your results in this activity, what do you think happens when a cold air mass meets a warm air mass?

   ____

   - Which air mass is pushed upward?

   ____

Name ______________________ Class ______________ Date ____________

Explore Activity

DATASHEET B

The Meeting of Air Masses

In this activity, you will model what happens when two air masses that have different temperature characteristics meet.

SAFETY INFORMATION

PROCEDURE

1. Pour **500 mL of water** into a **beaker.** Pour **500 mL of cooking oil** into a **second beaker.** The water represents a dense, cold air mass. The cooking oil represents a less dense, warm air mass.
2. Predict what would happen to the two liquids if you tried to mix them.

____

____

3. Pour the contents of both beakers into a **clear, plastic, rectangular container** at the same time from opposite ends of the container.
4. Observe the interaction of the oil and water.

ANALYSIS

5. What happens when the liquids meet?

____

____

6. Does the prediction that you made in step 2 match your results?

____

____

7. Using your results, hypothesize what happens when a cold air mass meets a warm air mass.

____

____

____

Explore Activity

DATASHEET C

The Meeting of Air Masses

In this activity, you will model what happens when two air masses that have different temperature characteristics meet.

SAFETY INFORMATION

PROCEDURE

1. Pour **500 mL of water** into a **beaker**. Pour **500 mL of cooking oil** into a **second beaker.** The water represents a cold air mass. The cooking oil represents a warm air mass.
2. Predict what would happen to the two liquids if you tried to mix them.

   ____

   ____

3. Pour the contents of both beakers into a **clear, plastic, rectangular container** at the same time from opposite ends of the container.
4. Observe the interaction of the oil and water.

ANALYSIS

5. What happens when the liquids interact? Is one liquid less dense than the other? If so, which one?

   ____

   ____

   ____

6. Does the prediction that you made in step 2 match your results?

   ____

   ____

7. Based on your results, hypothesize what happens when a cold air mass meets a warm air mass.

   ____

   ____

   ____

Quick Lab

DATASHEET

Reaching the Dew Point

Teacher Notes

This activity helps students understand precipitation (covers standard 6.4.e). Clean soup cans (check for sharp edges first) or glass beakers will work in place of the plastic container for this activity.

MATERIALS

For each group

- container, plastic
- ice cubes (1 or 2)
- water, room temperature

Name ______________________ Class ______________ Date ______________

Quick Lab

DATASHEET A

Reaching the Dew Point

PROCEDURE

1. Fill a **plastic container**, such as a cup, with **room-temperature water.**
   - The water level should be near the top of the cup.
2. Look at the outside of the container.
   - What can you see happening to the outside of the cup?

   ____

   ____

3. Add **one or two ice cubes** to the container of water.
4. Watch the outside of the container for any changes.
5. What happened to the outside of the container?

   ____

   ____

6. Where did the liquid come from? Explain your answer.

   ____

   ____

   ____

7. When the water in the container was cooled, the air outside the glass reached the dew point.
   - Explain how the cooling of the water inside the glass causes the air outside the glass to reach the dew point.

   ____

   ____

   ____

   ____

   ____

   ____

Name ______________________ Class ______________ Date ____________

Quick Lab

DATASHEET B

Reaching the Dew Point

PROCEDURE

1. Pour **room-temperature water** into a **plastic container,** such as a drinking cup, until the water level is near the top of the cup.
2. Observe the outside of the container, and record your observations.

____

____

____

3. Add **one or two ice cubes** to the container of water.
4. Watch the outside of the container for any changes.
5. What happened to the outside of the container?

____

____

6. Where did the liquid come from? Explain your answer.

____

____

____

____

7. Explain how the cooling of the water inside the glass causes the air outside the glass to reach the dew point.

____

____

____

____

____

Name ______________________ Class ______________ Date ____________

Quick Lab

DATASHEET C

Reaching the Dew Point

PROCEDURE

1. Pour **room temperature water** into a **plastic container,** such as a drinking cup, until the water level is near the top of the cup.

2. Observe the outside of the container, and record your observations.

____

____

3. Add **one or two ice cubes** to the container of water.

4. Watch the outside of the container for any changes.

5. What happened to the outside of the container?

____

____

6. Where did the liquid come from? Explain your answer.

____

____

7. Explain how the cooling of the water inside the glass causes the air outside the glass to reach the dew point. What type of energy transfer was involved?

____

____

____

____

____

____

Quick Lab

DATASHEET

Modeling a Front

Teacher Notes

This activity helps students understand weather fronts (covers standard 6.4.e).

MATERIALS

For each group

- bottle opener
- ice cube
- jar, glass, with metal lid
- water, hot, 1 mL

SAFETY CAUTION

Remind students to review all safety cautions and icons before beginning this activity.

Name ______________________________ Class ______________ Date ____________

Quick Lab

DATASHEET A

Modeling a Front

SAFETY INFORMATION

PROCEDURE

1. Use a **bottle opener** to punch one or two holes into the **metal lid** of a **glass jar**.
2. Pour **1 mL of hot water** into the jar.
   - Place the lid on the jar.
3. Place an **ice cube** over the holes in the lid.
   - Make sure the holes are completely covered.
4. Watch the changes that occur within the jar.
5. Draw a diagram of what you observe in the jar.
   - In your diagram, show:
     - the warm air mass
     - the cold air mass
     - the front where the two air masses meet

6. How do you know where the front is located?

____

____

____

____

Name ______________________ Class ______________ Date ______________

Quick Lab

DATASHEET B

Modeling a Front

SAFETY INFORMATION

PROCEDURE

1. Use a **bottle opener** to punch one or two holes into the **metal lid** of a **glass jar.**
2. Pour **1 mL of hot water** into the jar. Place the lid on the jar.
3. Place an **ice cube** over the holes in the lid. Make sure the holes are completely covered.
4. Observe the changes that occur within the jar.
5. Draw a diagram of what you observe in the jar.

6. In your diagram, label the location of the warm air mass, the cold air mass, and the front where the two air masses meet. How do you know where the front is located?

Name ______________________ Class ______________ Date ____________

Quick Lab

DATASHEET C

Modeling a Front

SAFETY INFORMATION

PROCEDURE

1. Use a **bottle opener** to punch one or two holes into the **metal lid** of a **glass jar**.
2. Pour **1 mL of hot water** into the jar. Place the lid on the jar.
3. Place an **ice cube** over the holes in the lid. Make sure the holes are completely covered.
4. Observe the changes that occur within the jar.
5. Draw a diagram of what you observe in the jar.

6. In your diagram, label the location of the warm air mass, the cold air mass, and the front where the two air masses meet. Explain how you determined the location of the front.

____

____

____

____

Quick Lab

DATASHEET

A Cool Breeze

Teacher Notes

This activity helps students understand how large bodies of water affect climate (covers standard 6.4.e).

MATERIALS

For each group

- cup
- fan, paper
- ice cubes (2)
- thermometer
- water

SAFETY CAUTION

Remind students to review all safety cautions and icons before beginning this activity.

Name ______________________ Class ______________ Date ____________

Quick Lab

DATASHEET A

A Cool Breeze

SAFETY INFORMATION

PROCEDURE

1. Hold a **thermometer** next to the top edge of a **cup** of **water** containing **two ice cubes.**
   - Record the temperature next to the cup.

   ____

2. Have your lab partner fan the surface of the cup with a **paper fan** for about one minute.
   - Record the temperature again.

   ____

3. Did the air temperature get cooler, or did it stay the same?

   ____

   - Why do you think the air temperature changed?

   ____

4. How does this model show how a large body of water, such as a lake or ocean, affects climate?

   ____

   ____

   ____

   ____

   ____

Name ______________________ Class ______________ Date ____________

Quick Lab

DATASHEET B

A Cool Breeze

SAFETY INFORMATION

PROCEDURE

1. Hold a **thermometer** next to the top edge of a **cup of water** containing **two ice cubes.** Record the temperature next to the cup.

____

2. Have your lab partner fan the surface of the cup with a **paper fan**. Record the temperature again.

____

3. Did the temperature change? Why or why not?

____

____

____

____

4. Explain how this activity models how a large body of water affects climate.

____

____

____

____

____

____

____

Name ______________ Class ______________ Date ______________

Quick Lab

DATASHEET C

A Cool Breeze

SAFETY INFORMATION

PROCEDURE

1. Hold a **thermometer** next to the top edge of a **cup of water** containing **two ice cubes.** Record the temperature next to the cup.

2. Have your lab partner fan the surface of the cup with a **paper fan**. Record the temperature again.

3. Did the temperature change? Why or why not?

4. Based on what you learned in this activity, how might large bodies of water affect the climate of an area?

Quick Lab

DATASHEET

Hot Stuff

Teacher Notes

This activity helps students understand how different materials absorb heat (covers standard 6.4.b). Students need to go outside to collect the data for this activity.

MATERIALS

For each group

- thermometer

Name ______________________ Class ______________ Date ____________

Quick Lab

DATASHEET A

Hot Stuff

PROCEDURE

1. In midafternoon, use a **thermometer** to measure the air temperature over a grassy field.
   - Take the temperature 1 m above the surface.
   - Make sure to shield the thermometer from direct sunlight.

2. Measure the air temperature over a parking lot.
   - Take the measurement 1 m above the surface.
   - Make sure the thermometer is not directly in the sunlight.

3. Was the temperature the same in both locations?

____

   - Which location was warmer?

____

   - How would you explain the difference in the results?

____

____

4. A builder is designing a new store and wants to keep cooling costs low. Would you suggest that the builder surround the store with trees and grass, or with a parking lot?

____

   - Explain your answer.

____

____

____

____

____

Name ______________________ Class ______________ Date ______________

Quick Lab

DATASHEET B

Hot Stuff

PROCEDURE

1. In midafternoon, use a **thermometer** to measure the air temperature over a grassy field or other vegetated area. Make sure to shield the thermometer from sunlight.
2. Measure the air temperature over a parking lot. Take the measurement at the same height above the surface. Make sure the thermometer is not directly in the sunlight.
3. How did the results differ between locations? How would you explain the difference in the results?

____

____

____

____

____

____

____

4. What suggestion for how to keep cooling costs low would you give to someone who is building a new store? Explain your answer.

____

____

____

____

____

____

____

____

Name ________________________ Class ______________ Date ____________

Quick Lab

DATASHEET C

Hot Stuff

PROCEDURE

1. In mid-afternoon, use a **thermometer** to measure the air temperature over a grassy field or other vegetated area. Make sure to shield the thermometer from sunlight.
2. Measure the air temperature over a parking lot. Take the measurement at the same height above the surface. Make sure the thermometer is not directly in the sunlight.
3. How did the results differ between locations? What factors could account for a difference in temperature readings?

____

____

4. What suggestion for how to keep cooling costs low would you give to someone who is building a new store? Explain your answer.

____

____

____

____

- What effect could large areas of pavement surrounding new housing, or loss of trees or other vegetation in an area, have on temperature?

____

____

____

____

____

____

____

____

Skills Practice Lab

DATASHEET

Convection Currents

Teacher Notes

This lab has students demonstrate how convection currents distribute heat in the atmosphere (covers standards 6.3.c, 6.4.d, and 6.4.e).

TEACHER TESTED & APPROVED

Dan Judnick
Bernal
Intermediate School
San Jose, California

TIME REQUIRED

One 45-minute class period

LAB RATINGS

Easy ← 1 2 3 4 → Hard

Teacher Prep–2
Student Set-Up–3
Concept Level–3
Clean Up–1

MATERIALS

The materials listed on this page are enough for groups of 2–4 students. You may want to have your first class make the boxes for you to reuse with the rest of your classes.

SAFETY CAUTION

Remind students to review all safety cautions and icons before beginning this activity.

LAB NOTES

You may wish to build a model of the convection chamber before class to show students. Their building process may go faster if they have a real model.

If chimney lamps are not available, you can create your own chimney lamps out of plastic drink bottles that have the bottoms cut out.

The cardboard boxes may be difficult to cut. You can prepare precut boxes if you prefer.

If sturdy tongs are not available, students may use an insulated mitt to place the steaming hot water into the box.

You may want to provide a metal can with a lid for extinguishing the smoking incense stick.

Name ____________________ Class ____________ Date ____________

Skills Practice Lab

DATASHEET A

Convection Currents

Why are some days windy and some days not windy? Where does wind come from? Wind is the movement of air that is caused by convection currents. Convection currents are caused by the uneven heating of Earth's surface. Convection currents distribute heat throughout the atmosphere and affect weather all around the world. In this lab you will create your own convection current.

OBJECTIVES

Demonstrate how convection currents distribute heat in the atmosphere.

Describe how the movement of air affects weather.

MATERIALS

- box, cardboard, volume of a 10-gallon aquarium
- chimney lamps (2)
- compass, drawing
- cup, glass
- incense
- knife, utility
- matches
- pencil
- plastic wrap
- tape, wide, transparent
- tongs

SAFETY INFORMATION

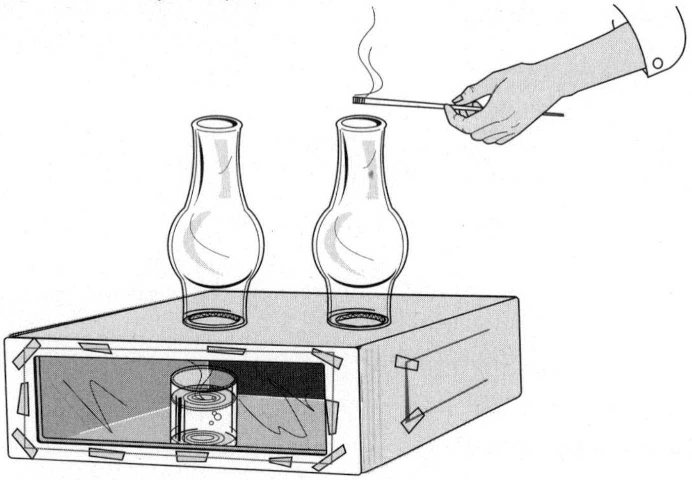

PROCEDURE

1. Cut off the flaps to the opening of your cardboard box.
2. Position the box so that the opening is the side that faces you.

3. Use the utility knife to cut out a flap that can be opened and closed on the side of the box that is next to the opening.
- The flap should be about half of the area of the side.
- Use the figure on the previous page as a model.

4. Open a drawing compass to a radius that is slightly smaller than the base of a chimney lamp.
- On the top of the box, at opposite ends, draw two circles using the drawing compass.

5. Use a utility knife to cut out the circles you drew on the box.

6. Cover the opening that you created in step 1 with plastic wrap.
- Use transparent tape to secure and seal the plastic wrap.

7. With tape, secure the chimney lamps over the holes in the top of the box.

8. Place a cup of steaming, hot water into the box through the closable flap.
- Use a pair of tongs to lift and move the cup,
- Position the cup under one of the chimney lamps.
- Close the flap carefully so that no draft is created inside the box.

9. Light an incense stick and immediately blow it out.
- Hold the smoking end of the incense stick over the mouth of the lamp chimney that does not have the cup of hot water under it.

10. Draw a diagram of what you observe.
- Use arrows to show the direction of movement.
- Use the space provided below.

ANALYZE THE RESULTS

11. Analyzing Data Describe how the smoke moved.

____

____

2. **Analyzing Results** How would you describe the movement of the air above the hot cup of water?

____

- Why does the air move in this direction?

____

13. **Explaining Events** What is causing the movement of air in your model?

____

____

DRAW CONCLUSIONS

14. **Interpreting Information** How does your model show how air moves in the atmosphere?

____

BIG IDEA QUESTION

15. **Drawing Conclusions** How do convection currents affect weather?

____

____

- If convection did not occur in the atmosphere, how do you think weather would be changed here on Earth?

____

____

____

____

Name ______________________ Class ______________ Date ______________

Skills Practice Lab

DATASHEET B

Convection Currents

Why are some days windy and some days not windy? Where does wind come from? Wind is the movement of air that is caused by convection currents. Convection currents are caused by the uneven heating of Earth's surface. Convection currents distribute heat throughout the atmosphere and affect weather all around the world. In this lab, you will create your own convection current.

OBJECTIVES

Demonstrate how convection currents distribute heat in the atmosphere.

Describe how the movement of air affects weather.

MATERIALS

- box, cardboard, volume of a 10-gallon aquarium
- chimney lamps (2)
- compass, drawing
- cup, glass
- incense
- knife, utility
- matches
- pencil
- plastic wrap
- tape, wide, transparent
- tongs

SAFETY INFORMATION

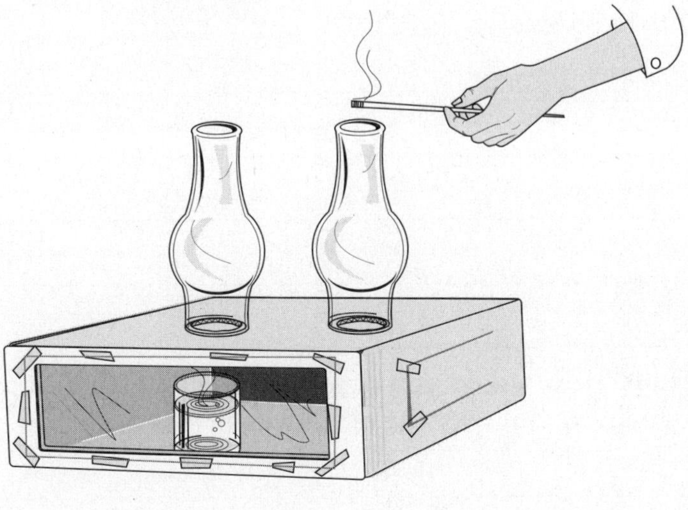

PROCEDURE

1. Cut off the flaps to the opening of your cardboard box.
2. Position the box so that the opening is the side that faces you.
3. Use the utility knife to cut out a flap that can be opened and closed on the side of the box that is next to the opening. The flap should be about half of the area of the side, as shown in the figure above.

4. Open a drawing compass to a radius that is slightly smaller than the base of a chimney lamp. Use the compass to draw two circles on top of the box, at opposite ends of the box.

5. Use a utility knife to cut out the circles you drew on the box.

6. Cover the opening that you created in step 1 with plastic wrap. Use transparent tape to secure and seal the plastic wrap.

7. With tape, secure the chimney lamps over the holes in the top of the box.

8. Using a pair of tongs, place a cup of steaming, hot water into the box through the closable flap. Position the cup under one of the chimney lamps. Close the flap carefully so that no draft is created inside the box.

9. Light an incense stick, and immediately blow it out. Then, hold the smoking end of the incense stick over the mouth of the chimney lamp that does not have the cup of hot water under it.

10. Draw a diagram of what you observe.

ANALYZE THE RESULTS

11. Analyzing Data Describe the movement of the smoke.

____

____

____

____

____

12. Analyzing Results How would you describe the movement of the air above the hot cup of water? Explain why the air moves in this direction.

____

____

____

____

____

13. Explaining Events What is powering the movement of air in your model?

____

____

____

____

____

DRAW CONCLUSIONS

14. Interpreting Information How does your model relate to the movement of air in the atmosphere?

____

____

____

____

____

____

____

BIG IDEA QUESTION

15. Drawing Conclusions How do convection currents affect weather? What would weather on Earth be like if convection currents did not occur in the atmosphere?

____

____

____

____

____

____

____

____

Name ______________________ Class ______________ Date ____________

Skills Practice Lab

DATASHEET C

Convection Currents

Why are some days windy and some days not windy? Where does wind come from? Wind is the movement of air that is caused by convection currents. Convection currents are caused by the uneven heating of Earth's surface. Convection currents distribute heat throughout the atmosphere and affect weather all around the world. In this lab you will create your own convection current.

OBJECTIVES

Demonstrate how convection currents distribute heat in the atmosphere.

Describe how the movement of air affects weather.

MATERIALS

- box, cardboard, volume of a 10-gallon aquarium
- chimney lamps (2)
- compass, drawing
- cup, glass
- incense
- knife, utility
- matches
- pencil
- plastic wrap
- tape, wide, transparent
- tongs

SAFETY INFORMATION

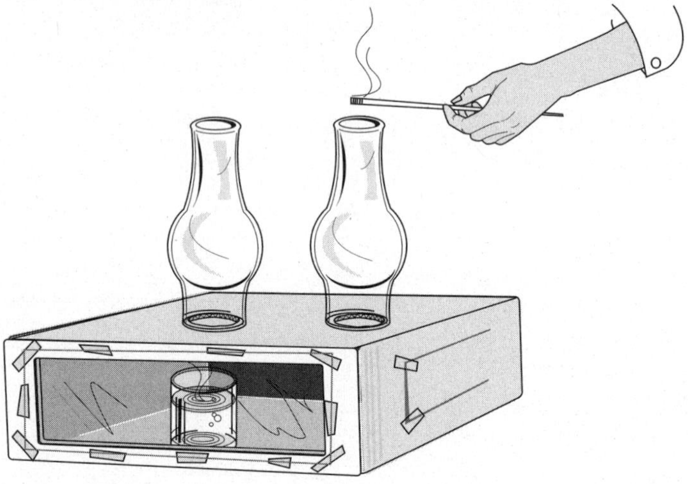

PROCEDURE

1. Cut off the flaps to the opening of your cardboard box.

2. Position the box so that the opening is the side that faces you.

3. Use the utility knife to cut out a flap that can be opened and closed on the side of the box that is next to the opening. The flap should be about half of the area of the side. The setup is illustrated by the figure on the previous page.
4. Open a drawing compass to a radius that is slightly smaller than the base of a chimney lamp. Use the compass to draw two circles on top of the box, at opposite ends of the box.
5. Use a utility knife to cut out the circles you drew on the box.
6. Cover the opening that you created in step 1 with plastic wrap. Use transparent tape to secure and seal the plastic wrap.
7. With tape, secure the chimney lamps over the holes in the top of the box.
8. Using a pair of tongs, place a cup of steaming, hot water into the box through the closable flap. Position the cup under one of the chimney lamps. Close the flap carefully so that no draft is created inside the box.
9. Light an incense stick and immediately blow it out. Then, hold the smoking end of the incense stick over the mouth of the lamp chimney that does not have the cup of hot water under it.
10. Draw a diagram of what you observe.

ANALYZE THE RESULTS

11. **Analyzing Data** Describe the movement of the smoke.

____

____

____

12. **Analyzing Processes** How would you describe the movement of the air above the hot cup of water? Explain why the air moves in this direction.

____

____

____

____

13. Identifying Relationships What is powering the movement of air in your model?

____

____

DRAW CONCLUSIONS

14. Interpreting Information The model you made shows convection currents. Use the model to explain why winds occur.

____

____

____

____

BIG IDEA QUESTION

15. Drawing Conclusions How do convection currents affect weather? What would weather on Earth be like if convection currents did not occur in the atmosphere? Consider temperature and moisture in your response.

____

____

____

____

____

____

____

____

____

Science Skills Activity

DATASHEET

Collecting Weather Data

Teacher Notes

This activity will walk students through the processes of data collection, data recording, and graphing. Students will use scientific procedures and equipment to collect and record data (covers standard 6.7.b). Students should be reminded that data collection should be taken at the same time and place every day in order to draw proper conclusions from the data.

MATERIALS

For each group

- barometer
- thermometer

Science Skills Activity

DATASHEET

Collecting Weather Data

INVESTIGATION AND EXPERIMENTATION

6.7.b Select and use appropriate tools and technology (including calculators, computers, balances, spring scales, microscopes, and binoculars) to perform tests, collect data, and display data.

TUTORIAL

Scientists use a variety of instruments to collect data. The meteorologists then analyze the relationships between the data and make predictions about the weather.

1. **Making a Data Table** On a piece of graph paper, make a chart like the one shown below. Record today's date above the first two columns labeled "A.M." and "P.M."

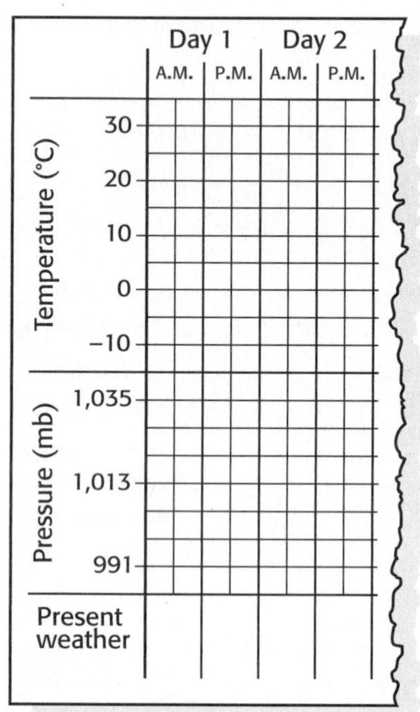

2. **Measuring Temperature** Place a thermometer in the shade where it is not exposed to precipitation. Wait at least 3 minutes. Then, read the temperature. Plot a point for that temperature on your chart.
3. **Measuring Atmospheric Pressure** Use a barometer to measure the atmospheric pressure to the nearest tenth of a millibar. Plot a point for the atmospheric pressure on your chart.
4. **Measuring Weather Conditions** Observe the present weather conditions, and record them in your chart. For example, if there is a light rain outside, write *drizzle* in your chart.

YOU TRY IT!

Procedure

Identify weather patterns and make weather predictions by following these steps.

1. On a piece of graph paper, create a fresh chart like the one above.
2. Twice daily for a week, at about the same time every day (about 10 hours apart), measure and record the temperature, atmospheric pressure, and weather conditions.
3. Use the data to make two graphs of changing temperature and atmospheric pressure. Do so by connecting the points for temperature with one smooth line and the points for atmospheric pressure with a second smooth line.

Analysis

4. **Inferring Relationships** In general, what is the relationship between temperature and atmospheric pressure?

____

____

____

____

____

5. **Drawing Conclusions** Did you notice any relationships between the atmospheric pressure and the weather conditions? If so, describe the relationships.

____

____

____

____

____

6. **Drawing Conclusions** How do the relationships between certain weather variables help you predict the weather?

____

____

____

____

____

Answer Key

Directed Reading A

SECTION: WATER IN THE AIR

1. C
2. D
3. C
4. dew point
5. vapor pressure
6. humidity
7. B
8. A
9. B
10. A
11. C
12. B
13. C
14. D
15. A
16. B
17. B
18. A

SECTION: FRONTS AND WEATHER

1. B
2. A
3. B
4. A
5. B
6. D
7. C
8. A
9. B
10. D
11. A
12. C
13. A
14. B
15. D
16. C
17. C
18. B
19. D
20. lightning
21. thunder
22. A
23. B
24. B
25. D
26. D
27. A
28. C
29. B
30. B

SECTION: WHAT IS CLIMATE?

1. B
2. C
3. C
4. D
5. A
6. C
7. D
8. A
9. elevation
10. rain-shadow effect
11. topography
12. D
13. C
14. B
15. C
16. A
17. A
18. C

SECTION: CHANGES IN CLIMATE

1. B
2. B
3. C
4. B
5. D
6. A
7. C
8. C
9. D
10. B
11. C
12. A
13. D
14. D
15. B
16. D

Directed Reading B

SECTION: WATER IN THE AIR

1. weather
2. the sun's energy
3. The water cycle is the movement of water between the atmosphere, the land, and the oceans.

4. D
5. B
6. C
7. A
8. the rates of evaporation and condensation
9. The air is saturated with water molecules.
10. liquid water droplets
11. The thin-film polymer in the sensor absorbs water vapor as the relative humidity in the air rises and releases water vapor as the relative humidity drops. As the amount of water in the film changes, the electrical properties of the film change. The amount of stored electric charge is measured and quickly converted into a relative humidity reading.
12. B
13. when the air has a relative humidity of 100%
14. The air next to the glass drops to below the dew point, and the condensation rate exceeds the evaporation rate.
15. water droplets that form on grass or other things near the ground at night when the air cools to below the dew point
16. a collection of millions of tiny water droplets or ice crystals suspended in the air
17. by their shape and their altitude
18. stratus clouds, cumulus clouds, cirrus clouds
19. precipitation
20. rain, snow, sleet, hail

SECTION: FRONTS AND WEATHER

1. the interaction of air masses
2. air mass
3. B
4. C
5. B
6. C
7. D
8. A
9. cold front: heavy rain or snow followed by cooler weather; warm front: drizzly rain and then clear, warm weather; occluded front: cool temperatures and large amounts of rain and snow; stationary front: many days of cloudy, wet weather
10. cyclone
11. anticyclones
12. It causes stormy weather.
13. It brings dry, clear weather.
14. D
15. warm and moist air near Earth's surface and an unstable atmosphere
16. lightning
17. thunder
18. B
19. A funnel cloud becomes a tornado when it touches down on Earth's surface.
20. hurricane
21. over warm, tropical oceans in the areas between 5° and 20° north latitude and 5° and 20° south latitude
22. from the evaporation and condensation of water vapor
23. Hurricanes lose energy over colder waters. When a hurricane approaches California, the storm quickly dies out over the cold California coastal waters.
24. hail, lightning, high winds, tornadoes, flash floods
25. flash flooding
26. storm surge
27. move to higher ground

SECTION: WHAT IS CLIMATE?

1. A
2. climate
3. temperature and amount of precipitation
4. latitude, wind patterns, locations of mountains and large bodies of water, nearness to ocean currents
5. distance north or south, measured in degrees, from the equator
6. The higher the latitude is, the colder the climate tends to be. Therefore, the temperatures at the poles are very low.
7. the curve of Earth
8. Seasons happen because Earth is tilted on its axis at a 23.5° angle, which affects how much solar energy an area receives as Earth moves around the sun.
9. convection currents caused by an uneven heating of Earth's surface

10. Answers may vary. Sample answer: Winds carry solar energy to and from different locations, which changes the temperatures of the locations. Winds also carry evaporated water from the ocean surface to other places where it may condense and fall as precipitation.
11. topography
12. elevations
13. As air rises to pass over a mountain, the air cools, which causes clouds to form and precipitation to fall.
14. Large bodies of water, such as the ocean, absorb and release heat more slowly than land does.
15. surface currents
16. the California current
17. A polar bear is adapted to one climate and is not able to live in another climate.
18. tropical, temperate, polar
19. There are several kinds of climates because of differences in topography, winds, ocean currents, and geography.

SECTION: CHANGES IN CLIMATE

1. because climates change slowly
2. human activity and natural factors
3. that Earth's climate has been much warmer and much colder than it is today
4. ice age
5. glacial and interglacial periods
6. because a large amount of ocean water is frozen
7. The Milankovitch theory explains that changes in Earth's orbit and in the tilt of Earth's axis cause ice ages.
8. how much solar radiation the continent receives
9. The flow of air and moisture around the globe changes.
10. Answers may vary. Sample answer: The amount of energy that the sun emits changes over time. Sometimes the sun produces a low percentage of high-energy radiation, and other times it produces more high-energy radiation. These variations can cause slight changes in Earth's climate.
11. asteroid
12. debris
13. Answers may vary. Sample answer: The debris from a crashing asteroid's impact could have blocked sunlight from reaching Earth, lowering air temperatures. Plants wouldn't get the sunlight they needed to grow, and animals therefore would have had no food to survive.
14. Volcanic eruptions send large amounts of dust, ash, and smoke into the atmosphere, which act as a shield, blocking solar energy.
15. global warming
16. B
17. an increase in carbon dioxide in the atmosphere
18. Answers may vary. Sample answer: Icecaps would melt and cause flooding; deserts might receive even less rainfall than normal; crops would be harmed by changes in weather patterns.

Vocabulary and Section Summary A

SECTION: WATER IN THE AIR

1. weather: the short-term state of the atmosphere, including temperature, humidity, precipitation, wind, and visibility
2. humidity: the amount of water vapor in the air
3. dew point: at constant pressure and water vapor content, the temperature at which the rate of condensation equals the rate of evaporation
4. relative humidity: the ratio of the amount of water vapor in the air to the amount of water vapor needed to reach saturation at a given temperature
5. condensation: the change of state from a gas to a liquid
6. precipitation: any form of water that falls to Earth's surface from the clouds

SECTION: FRONTS AND WEATHER

1. air mass: a large body of air throughout which temperature and moisture content are similar
2. front: the boundary between air masses of different densities and usually different temperatures

3. cyclone: an area in the atmosphere that has lower pressure than the surrounding areas and has winds that spiral toward the center
4. lightning: an electric discharge that takes place between two oppositely charged surfaces, such as between a cloud and the ground, between two clouds, or between two parts of the same cloud
5. thunder: the sound caused by the rapid expansion of air along an electrical strike
6. tornado: a destructive, rotating column of air that has very high wind speeds and that may be visible as a funnel-shaped cloud

SECTION: WHAT IS CLIMATE?

1. climate: the average weather conditions in an area over a long period of time
2. latitude: the distance north or south from the equator; expressed in degrees
3. elevation: the height of an object above sea level
4. surface currents: a horizontal movement of ocean water that is caused by wind and that occurs at or near the ocean's surface

SECTION: CHANGES IN CLIMATE

1. ice age: a long period of climatic cooling during which the continents are glaciated repeatedly
2. global warming: a gradual increase in the average global temperature
3. greenhouse effect: when water vapor, carbon dioxide, and other gases absorb and reradiate thermal energy

Vocabulary and Section Summary B

SECTION: WATER IN THE AIR

1. relative humidity
2. precipitation
3. humidity
4. weather
5. condensation
6. dew point

SECTION: FRONTS AND WEATHER

12:34 pm: air mass, front, cyclone
1:21 pm: lightning, thunder
1:38 pm: tornado

SECTION: WHAT IS CLIMATE?

1. climate
2. weather
3. latitude
4. elevation
5. surface current
6. topography

S	U	R	F	A	C	E	C	U	R	R	E	N	T
A	V	W	B	S	T	B	L	U	A	E	I	O	O
P	E	W	T	W	S	M	I	N	F	G	M	A	P
C	L	I	S	P	E	A	M	X	E	I	B	T	O
P	E	H	M	N	A	A	A	A	M	L	K	G	G
H	V	B	A	R	O	H	T	Y	E	B	B	L	R
S	A	C	B	I	O	N	E	H	E	A	C	M	A
F	T	T	C	A	H	D	I	D	E	I	O	G	P
H	I	S	L	E	G	L	M	O	S	R	E	R	H
P	O	N	B	A	F	E	S	M	B	R	A	S	Y
N	N	D	M	E	D	U	T	I	T	A	L	F	G

SECTION: CHANGES IN CLIMATE

1. glacial periods
2. global warming
3. debris
4. greenhouse effect
5. ice ages
6. asteroid

Reinforcement

SEVERE WEATHER

Thunderstorm

Conditions: Sample answer: Thunderstorms occur in any climate where the air near Earth's surface is warm and moist and the atmosphere is unstable.
Formation: Sample answer: Warm, moist air rises rapidly in an unstable atmosphere. As warm air continues to rise, cumulus clouds grow into dark, cumulonimbus clouds.

Tornado

Conditions: Sample answer: Wind moves in two directions, causing a layer of air to begin to spin.
Formation: Sample answer: The spinning column of air is turned to a vertical position by strong updrafts. A funnel cloud appears and touches the ground.

Hurricane
Conditions: Sample answer: Hurricanes form in tropical climates. They form between 5° and 20° north and south latitude over warm, tropical oceans.
Formation: Sample answer: Hurricanes move over tropical waters. Winds traveling from two directions collide and rotate over an area of low pressure.

Critical Thinking

1. Answers may vary. Sample answer: No, the Internet is not always a reliable source of scientific fact. For example, anyone can post his or her views in chat rooms. These views are usually based on personal opinion, not scientific fact.
2. Dr. Betty has the most scientific viewpoint. Unlike the others, she refers to a source of scientific data to back up her argument.
3. Answers may vary. Sample answer: Yes, Dr. Betty may be biased because her job security may be based on global warming research.
4. Answers may vary. Sample answer: Although carbon dioxide is a natural part of our environment, atmospheric levels of it have been increasing for a century, probably due to the increased burning of fuels for transportation and industry. Also, the burning of forests to clear land for farming also may increase carbon dioxide.
5. Answers may vary. Sample answer: Web sites sponsored by universities or nonprofit organizations dedicated to scientific research would be more reliable and objective.

SciLinks Activity

1. oceans, lakes, plants
2. It turns into liquid water droplets that collect and form a cloud.
3. Rainwater runs off into storm sewers, lakes, and rivers and eventually seeps into the ground.
4. factors such as solar radiation, the temperature, humidity, and wind
5. the ocean
6. Plants return water to the atmosphere by releasing water through their leaves.
7. It means that warm, humid air rises, and cooler air flows downward.

Section Review

SECTION: WATER IN THE AIR

1. humidity
2. precipitation
3. Relative humidity is the ratio of the amount of water vapor in the air to the amount of water vapor needed to reach saturation at a given temperature.
4. Liquid water evaporates, changing into water vapor. The water vapor condenses to form clouds when the temperature drops. When water droplets in clouds become large enough, they fall to Earth's surface as precipitation. When precipitation falls to Earth, flows over land and into rivers, and eventually flows into the ocean, it is called *runoff*.
5. The dew point is the temperature at which the rate of condensation equals the rate of evaporation. Below the dew point, water that condenses from the air can accumulate on surfaces as water droplets.
6. The sun is the water cycle's energy source.
7. As the air drops to below the dew-point, the rate of condensation increases and exceeds the rate of evaporation.
8. cumulus
9. 2,000–3,000 m
10. The body of air that has a relative humidity of 97% is closer to its dew point because this body of air is closer to saturation.

SECTION: FRONTS AND WEATHER

1. thunderstorm
2. thunder
3. A cold front forms where cold air moves under warm air. A warm air front is where warm air moves over cold air.
4. Energy from the sun heats the ocean water and causes the water to evaporate. The evaporation adds moisture to the air, which leads to thunderstorms that produce a large vortex.

5. Lightning is caused by an electrical discharge that takes place between two oppositely charged surfaces, such as between a cloud and the ground.
6. A cold front brings cooler weather. A warm front usually brings drizzly rain.
7. Floods can affect people by causing property damage and death.
8. The movement of warm air as it rises, cools, and reaches its dew point helps form dark, cumulonimbus clouds in thunderstorms. The heat flow when lightning strikes and superheats the air causes the thunder in thunderstorms.
9. Cyclones are areas of low pressure. Anticyclones are areas of high pressure. Cyclones can cause rainy, stormy weather. Anticyclones cause dry, clear weather.
10. When a hurricane moves over land, it loses its energy and dies out because there is no longer ocean water to evaporate and fuel the storm.
11. Severe weather can cause floods if there are heavy rains. Hurricanes can also cause floods through storm surges, which are rises in sea level caused by strong winds.
12. Sample answer: Just as flooding can destroy human homes and endanger lives, flooding can destroy the homes and endanger the lives of plants and animals.
13. The front is moving to the right. I can tell because that is the direction in which the fronts are moving.
14. The illustration represents a warm front.
15. The air masses move because different air masses have different temperature and therefore have different densities. The differences in density cause air masses to move relative to other air masses. If air masses did not move, there would not be changes in weather. Fronts do not form between two air masses that have the same temperature because the air masses have the same density and therefore the air masses will mix and form one air mass.

SECTION: WHAT IS CLIMATE?

1. Sample answer: Climate is the average weather conditions in an area over a long period of time. Latitude is the distance north or south from the equator, expressed in degrees. Elevation is the height of surface landforms above sea level. Surface currents are streamlike movements of water at or near the surface of the ocean.
2. Topography can influence wind patterns and the transfer of energy in an area, which affects the climate of the area.
3. Weather is the condition of the atmosphere at a certain time. Climate is the average weather conditions in an area over a long period of time.
4. The five factors that affect climate are latitude, winds, topography, proximity to large bodies of water, and ocean currents.
5. The sun's rays hit areas with 0° latitude at a direct 90° angle. At this angle, solar energy is concentrated on a small area. An area at 45° latitude receives the sun's rays at a lesser angle, so the same amount of solar energy is spread over a larger area than at 0° latitude. Because the energy at 45° latitude is less concentrated, the climate has lower temperatures than the climate of the area at 0° latitude does.
6. Winds, which are a result of convection currents, carry solar energy from one place to another.
7. The southern tip of South America is at a high latitude. Therefore, the tip of South America has a cold climate and experiences short summers and long winters.
8. Australia has summer during the months of December, January, and February because Australia is in the Southern Hemisphere, which is tilted toward the sun during these months.,
9. If Earth were not tilted on its axis, no area on Earth would experience seasonal change. All areas on Earth would have more moderate temperatures all year long.

10. Climate cannot be classified only by latitude because many other factors, such as topography, global winds, proximity to large bodies of water, and ocean currents, affect climate.
11. City A is more likely to have the largest yearly temperature range because it is not near a large body of water that would moderate its temperature changes.
12. City A is more likely to have a dry climate because it is not on the windward side of the mountain.
13. The climate of City A will be a dry, desert climate. The climate of City B will be moist, and City B will have more rain or snow than City A.
14. Sample answer: Because California is at a middle latitude, it experiences some change of seasons throughout the year. The winds and mountains of California create a rain-shadow effect. Therefore, areas east of mountain ranges have desert climates. The cold California ocean current along the West Coast keeps the temperatures along California's coast cooler than temperatures inland.

SECTION: CHANGES IN CLIMATE

1. Sample answers: An ice age is a period of climatic cooling during which the continents are glaciated repeatedly. Global warming is a gradual increase in the average global temperature. The greenhouse effect is the process by which water vapor, carbon dioxide, and other gases absorb and reradiate thermal energy.
2. The Milankovitch theory explains how variations in Earth's orbit, tilt, and wobble affect the amount or intensity of solar radiation that is received by Earth.
3. Factors that can affect the amount of solar energy that reaches Earth's surface are volcanic eruptions, impacts by large asteroids, the sun's cycle, and changes in Earth's orbit, tilt, and wobble.
4. An increase in global temperatures may cause polar icecaps to melt, causing sea levels to rise, which would cause flooding in coastal areas.
5. Factors that may cause changes in Earth's climate are changes in Earth's tilt, orbit, and wobble, plate tectonics, the sun's cycle, an asteroid impact, a volcanic eruption, and human activity.
6. The greenhouse effect warms Earth because gases in the atmosphere absorb heat. As a result, the heat stays in the atmosphere and keeps Earth warm.
7. The warming of Earth could have positive and negative effects on agriculture throughout the world. Colder climates would become warmer, which might improve the growth of some crops. Warm climates would become too warm, which might decrease precipitation in some areas. Some crops would die from drought.
8. Sample answer: I could decrease the amount of carbon dioxide that is released into the atmosphere by using less electricity. I could do this by turning off lights when I am not using them and by using only cold water to wash clothes.
9. 160 L $\div$ 4 L = 40; 40 $\times$ 9 kg = 360 kg of carbon dioxide in one month
10. No, short-term climate changes cannot be explained by changes in the tilt of Earth's axis because it takes 41,000 years for the angle of tilt to change from 24.5° to 22.2°.

Chapter Review

1. C
2. Relative humidity is the ratio of the amount of water vapor in the air to the amount of water vapor needed to reach saturation. Dew point is the temperature at which the rate of condensation equals the rate of evaporation.
3. Condensation is the process by which a gas becomes liquid. Precipitation is water in any form that falls to Earth's surface from the clouds.
4. An air mass is a large body of air that has similar temperature and moisture content throughout. A front is the boundary between two air masses.
5. Weather is the condition of the atmosphere at a certain time. Climate is the average weather conditions in an area over a long period of time.

6. Thunder is the sound caused by the rapid expansion of air along an electrical strike. Lightning is an electrical discharge that takes place between two oppositely charged surfaces or between two oppositely charged parts of the same cloud.
7. C
8. C
9. B
10. C
11. When the temperature drops below the dew point, the rate of condensation is greater than the rate of evaporation and net condensation occurs.
12. A stationary front generally causes many days of cloudy, rainy weather.
13. A hurricane forms when warm, moist air rises, condenses, and forms a group of thunderstorms over the tropical ocean waters. The thunderstorms produce a vortex that grows into a powerful hurricane as it is fueled by warm ocean water.
14. The water cycle is the movement of water between the atmosphere, the land, and the oceans. As the water moves through the cycle, it evaporates, condenses, and precipitates. These processes affect weather events, such as thunderstorms, hurricanes, and rain.
15. Winds carry heat to different locations, which causes temperature changes. Winds also carry water vapor, which can fall as precipitation.
16. Severe weather, such as flooding, tornadoes, and hurricanes, can damage crops, cars, and other property. It can also cause death.
17. Four factors that cause changes in weather are changes in air pressure, temperature, humidity, and movement of air.
18. The smallest number of tornadoes occurs between 4 A.M. and 8 A.M.
19. Students are more likely to experience a tornado while at home because most tornadoes occur between 4 P.M. and 8 P.M.
20. Answers may vary but should cover all requirements stated in the question.
21. An answer to this exercise can be found at the end of the Teacher Edition.
22. The amount of energy the sun produces changes over an 11-year cycle. Therefore, the amount of energy Earth receives from the sun changes, which affects temperatures and weather processes, such as the water cycle and wind patterns.
23. Yes, the relative humidity can stay the same because relative humidity is the ratio of the amount of water vapor in the air to the amount of water vapor needed to reach saturation at a given temperature. If the temperature and amount of water vapor change at a similar rate, the relative humidity will stay the same.
24. The climate on the western side of the Sierra Nevada is wetter than the climate on the eastern side is because the western side of the mountain range is on the windward side of a rain shadow.
25. The tilt of Earth's axis causes one hemisphere to receive more direct solar energy than the other hemisphere does. The hemisphere that receives more direct solar energy experiences the summer season, while the hemisphere that receives the less direct solar energy experiences the winter season.
26. As air of different densities moves in convection currents, this movement of air creates wind patterns.
27. If Earth were not tilted on its axis, the amount of solar energy each area on Earth received as Earth revolved around the sun would not change. Therefore, no area on Earth would experience seasons.
28. If the concentration of carbon dioxide in the air increased, global temperatures would be warmer. In many areas this would result in an increase in evaporation in the water cycle.
29. Human activity, such as burning fossil fuels for energy, releases carbon dioxide into the atmosphere. Carbon dioxide absorbs heat and increases global temperature, which affects world climate.

30. Two factors that affect climate in California are the Sierra Nevada mountain range and proximity to the ocean.
31. The Sierra Nevada mountain range causes a rain-shadow effect. Therefore, Barstow receives a small amount of annual precipitation.
32. $5/9 \times (47°F - 32) = 8°C$
33. Sample answer: If global temperatures were 5°C warmer, climate, including the amount of precipitation an area receives, may change. Plants and animals would have to adapt to a change in the availability of water, or they would die out.

Section Quizzes

SECTION: WATER IN THE AIR

1. D
2. B
3. E
4. C
5. A
6. B
7. B
8. C
9. D

SECTION: FRONTS AND WEATHER

1. B
2. D
3. A
4. C
5. D
6. C
7. A
8. B
9. C

SECTION: WHAT IS CLIMATE?

1. C
2. A
3. D
4. B
5. C
6. A
7. D
8. C
9. B

SECTION: CHANGES IN CLIMATE

1. B
2. A
3. C
4. C
5. A
6. D
7. B

Chapter Test A

1. D
2. A
3. D
4. B
5. A
6. D
7. A
8. A
9. B
10. C
11. B
12. C
13. A
14. D
15. B
16. D
17. C
18. B
19. A
20. condensation
21. greenhouse effect
22. global warming
23. elevation
24. ice age
25. front

Chapter Test B

1. C
2. B
3. A
4. E
5. F
6. D
7. C
8. D
9. D
10. D
11. D
12. B
13. A
14. B
15. D
16. A
17. B
18. C

19. A
20. D
21. C
22. D
23. B
24. C
25. A

Chapter Test C

1. relative humidity
2. weather
3. greenhouse effect
4. condensation
5. latitudes
6. precipitation
7. D
8. A
9. C
10. B
11. D
12. A
13. A
14. Answers may vary. Sample answer: Lightning forms when an electric discharge happens between a positively charged area and a negatively charged area, such as between a cloud and the ground or between two clouds or between two parts of the same cloud. When lightning strikes, the air along its path becomes superheated. The air vibrates and releases energy as sound waves. The result is thunder, which is the sound caused by the fast expansion of air along the lightning strike.
15. Answers may vary. Sample answer: During a storm, there is a rise in sea level, which forms a storm surge. The storm surge crashes onto shore, endangering lives and causing property damage.
16. Answers may vary. Sample answer: When air rises and cools to below the dew point, millions of tiny water droplets or ice crystals form a cloud.
17. Answers may vary. Sample answer: Hurricanes are fed by warm, moist air over the ocean. The North Atlantic Ocean is warmest in summer; by September, a large amount of heat has built up. So this is when the air over the oceans is warmest.
18. Answers may vary. Sample answer: During an ice age, ice forms in high latitudes and moves toward lower latitudes. There are periods of cold (glacial periods) and periods of warmth (interglacial periods). During a glacial period, large sheets of ice advance, get bigger, and cover a larger area. The sea level then drops.
19. Answers may vary. Sample answer: Milankovitch theory: This theory explains that changes in Earth's orbit and in the tilt of Earth's axis cause ice ages. Plate tectonics and continental drift: A continent's location relative to the equator and poles determines how much solar radiation it receives. A continent's location relative to oceans and other continents is also important. A continent deflects ocean currents. Also, when continents move, the flow of air and moisture around the globe changes. Sun's cycle: The sun produces different levels of high-energy radiation. These variations affect the amount of energy in Earth's systems, which cause slight changes in climate. Asteroid impact: Debris from asteroid impacts can block some sunlight from reaching Earth's surface, which would lower average temperatures. Volcanic eruptions: Ash, dust, and smoke from volcanic eruptions can block some of the sun's rays, resulting in the cooling of Earth's surface and atmosphere. Human activity: Increases in carbon dioxide caused by burning fossil fuels cause a slight rise in global temperatures.
20. **a.** air masses; **b.** front; **c.** hurricane; **d.** tornado; **e.** cyclone

Performance-Based Assessment

1. Sample answer: The water will form a separate "current" similar to the way currents are formed in the ocean by water that is warmer or colder than the general water temperature.
6. The colored water flowed to the bottom of the aquarium and remained there.
7. Large bodies of water, like oceans, can influence a region's climate. When warm waters flow over the top of colder ocean waters, the air at the ocean's surface is heated, causing warmer air temperatures in the region.
8. Answers may vary. Sample answer: Cold water from the northern Pacific Ocean is carried south by California ocean current. The cool current absorbs energy from the surrounding air and causes cooler temperatures. That is why temperatures along the West Coast are cooler than the temperatures inland.

Explore Activity

DATASHEET A

5. The two liquids separate. The oil rises to the top and sits on the surface of the water.
6. Answers may vary depending on predictions.
7. Sample answer: The two air masses would separate. The warm air mass would be pushed up by the cold air mass.

DATASHEET B

5. The oil rises to the top and sits on the surface of the water.
6. Answers may vary depending on predictions.
7. Sample answer: The warm air mass would be pushed up by the cold air mass.

DATASHEET C

5. The oil rises to the top and sits on the surface of the water. The oil is less dense than the water.
6. Answers may vary depending on predictions.
7. Sample answer: The warm air mass would be pushed up by the cold air mass.

Quick Lab: Reaching the Dew Point

DATASHEET A

2. Sample answer: The outside of the container did not change.
5. Liquid droplets formed on the outside of the container.
6. The air next to the cup cooled to below its dew point, and water vapor condensed on the cup.
7. The glass absorbed heat from the air through conduction. This caused the air near the glass to cool and condensation took place.

DATASHEET B

5. Liquid droplets formed on the outside of the container.
6. The air next to the cup cooled to below its dew point, and water vapor condensed on the cup.
7. The glass absorbed heat from the air through conduction. This process caused the air near the glass to cool, and condensation took place.

DATASHEET C

5. Liquid droplets formed on the outside of the container.
6. The air next to the cup cooled to below its dew point, and water vapor condensed on the cup.
7. The glass absorbed heat from the air through conduction. This caused the air near the glass to cool and condensation took place.

Quick Lab: Modeling a Front

DATASHEET A

5. Diagrams may vary but should include labels of fronts.
6. Sample answer: I know where the front is located because it is at the base of the cloud formation.

DATASHEET B

6. Diagrams may vary but should include labels of fronts. Sample answer: I know where the front is located because it is at the base of the cloud formation.

DATASHEET C

6. Diagrams may vary but should include labels of fronts. Sample answer: I determined the location of the front because I know it is at the base of the cloud formation.

Quick Lab: A Cool Breeze

DATASHEET A

3. The temperature decreased because the air traveling across the cup's surface was cooled by the ice water, which changed the air temperature.
4. The temperature of a large body of water affects the temperature of the air above the water. Thus, proximity to water affects the climate.

DATASHEET B

3. The temperature decreased because the air traveling across the cup's surface was cooled by the ice water, which changed the air temperature.
4. The temperature of a large body of water affects the temperature of the air above the water. Thus, proximity to water affects the climate.

DATASHEET C

3. The temperature decreased because the air traveling across the cup's surface was cooled by the ice water, which changed the air temperature.
4. The temperature of a large body of water would affect the temperature of the air above the water, thus affecting the climate.

Quick Lab: Hot Stuff

DATASHEET A

3. No. Temperature over the parking lot was higher than over the grassy field was. This is because the concrete that makes up the parking lot absorbs more heat than the grassy field does.
4. Someone building a new store could keep cooling costs down by planting trees and bushes around the store. A parking lot would create too much heat.

DATASHEET B

3. Temperature over the parking lot was higher than temperature over the grassy field was. The concrete that makes up the parking lot absorbs more heat than the grassy field does.
4. Someone building a new store could keep cooling costs down by planting trees and bushes around the store.

DATASHEET C

3. Temperature over the parking lot was higher than over the grassy field was. This is because the concrete that makes up the parking lot absorbs more heat than the grassy field does.
4. Someone building a new store could keep cooling costs down by planting trees and bushes around the store. Large areas of pavement, or the loss of trees or grassy areas, could cause the temperature in the surrounding area to rise.

Chapter Lab

DATASHEET A

11. The smoke from the incense stick went down through the chimney lamp into the box. It moved over the cup of hot water and up through the second chimney lamp.
12. The air above the hot cup of water rises. It moves in this direction because heated air becomes less dense and rises.
13. Heat from the hot cup of water creates a convection current that moves the air in the model.
14. Air movement in the model works in a way similar to the air movement in the atmosphere. In both, air moves because of differences in density caused by the heating of the air. In the model, the air is heated by the hot water. In the atmosphere, the air is heated by the sun.

15. Convection currents affect weather around the world because they transfer heat in the atmosphere. The transfer of heat from one area to another can lead to changes in the weather. These changes can be as subtle as a drop in the local temperature or as dramatic as a hurricane. If convection currents did not occur in the atmosphere, heat could not be transferred throughout the atmosphere and changes in weather would not occur.

DATASHEET B

11. The smoke from the incense stick went down through the chimney lamp into the box. It moved over the cup of hot water and up through the second chimney lamp.
12. The air above the cup of hot water rises because heated air becomes less dense and rises.
13. Heat from the hot cup of water creates a convection current that moves the air in the model.
14. Air movement in the model works in a similar way to how air moves in the atmosphere. Air moves because of differences in density caused by the heating of the air. In the model, the air is heated by the hot water. In the atmosphere, the air is heated by the sun.
15. Convection currents affect weather around the world because they transfer heat in the atmosphere. The transfer of heat from one area to another can lead to changes in the weather. These changes can be as subtle as a drop in the local temperature or as dramatic as a hurricane. If convection currents did not occur in the atmosphere, heat could not be transferred throughout the atmosphere and changes in weather would not occur.

DATASHEET C

11. The smoke from the incense stick went down through the chimney lamp into the box. It moved over the cup of hot water and up through the second chimney lamp.
12. The air above the hot cup of water rises because heated air becomes less dense and rises.
13. Heat from the hot cup of water creates a convection current that moves the air in the model.
14. Air movement in the model works in a similar way to how air moves in the atmosphere. In both, air moves because of differences in density caused by the heating of the air. In the model, the air is heated by the hot water. In the atmosphere, the air is heated by the sun.
15. Convection currents affect weather around the world because they transfer heat in the atmosphere. The transfer of heat from one area to another can lead to changes in the weather. These changes can be as subtle as a drop in the local temperature or as dramatic as a hurricane. If convection currents did not occur in the atmosphere, heat could not be transferred throughout the atmosphere and changes in weather would not occur, water vapor would not be moved, and the water cycle would not exist, and this would adversely affect life on the planet.

Science Skills Activity

DATASHEET

4. Usually, as temperature increases, pressure decreases.
5. Answers may vary. Sample answer: When the pressure is high, the skies are clear and the temperature is cool.
6. Answers may vary. Sample answer: If the pressure is falling, stormy weather is likely to come soon. If the pressure rises, fair weather can be predicted.